Angel Shadows

D.S Ingram

Angel Shadows

Islington casts long shadows over all its residents,

Born and bred,

Memories of the streets we used to tread.

Shadows that touched our lives,

Shadows some could not survive,

Some soft shadows,

Provided shelter from the glare of the sun,

Kissing your cheek when the day was done.

Some long shadows brought a chill to the warmth of the day,

Other darker shadows never seemed to go away.

Those were the shadows, the Angel shadows,

Would they protect you, or make you feel cold?

Would they reach out to awaken the pain?

Or stay by your side, as you grew old...

CHAPTER ONE

Jay Oakland cradled his new born son in his arms and looked tenderly down at him. He finally managed to drag his eyes away from his baby boy to look toward his wife Suzy. He thought she had never looked more beautiful. He was so in love with her. He felt like the luckiest man alive. He swallowed hard to try to dislodge the enormous lump that had formed in his throat. Their son was just an hour old. He beamed at Suzy. "Well even if I do say so myself," Jay said, after clearing his throat, "We sure know how to make beautiful children"

Suzy lay in her hard hospital bed and grinned back at the husband she adored and sighed happily. "He is gorgeous. What are we gonna call him, Jay? I was convinced we were gonna have another girl. I've only thought of girls names. I don't s'pose he'll be too chuffed when he gets older if we call him Mia. That was my favourite girl's name." Jay grinned at Suzy and his blue eyes shone. "What about calling him Jay junior?" Suzy ventured.

Jay shook his head. "No, I don't think so. One Jay Oakland is quite enough. I think we should call him Bobby after your dad. He'd like that, and he's always been so good to us."

Suzy's eyes immediately filled with tears. "Oh Jay, that's a lovely idea. My Dad'll be pleased as punch. I know why don't we call him Bobby Jay? I think it's got a nice ring to it. Then he'll have all my favourite men's names and my mum's initial is J. J for Joycie. She'll love that. I'm sure they'll appreciate the name Bobby. My brother was meant to be called Bobby, but they thought it would get a bit confusing having two Bobby's in the same house, so he's always been called by his proper name, Robert."

Jay considered it. "Bobby Jay? It sounds a bit like an extra from the Walton's TV series, but okay. If you want it, then welcome to the world little Bobby Jay" He kissed the baby's soft downy little head, then kissed Suzy.

Suzy's parents and her brother came to visit later. Her brother, Robert was carrying a white Steiff teddy bear with a blue bow around its neck. Robert had been to Hamleys toyshop in Regent Street especially to buy the bear. He had had the baby's date of birth embroidered on the ribbon. He adored his sister and was thrilled to become an uncle again. The bear had cost him a small fortune but he did not mind. It was only the best for his new baby nephew. He had also bought Amy, Suzy and Jay's daughter, a beautiful baby doll too. He did not want her to feel left out of things. He winked at Amy and gave her his present. She beamed at him and hugged the dolly. Robert smiled when he saw how pleased Amy was. He placed the bear wordlessly in the baby's cot and kissed his sister. "Well done, sis" he mumbled bashfully. He was always a man of few words thought Suzy, getting a bit over emotional. Suzy wiped her eyes on a Kleenex, and then held her arms open for her little daughter to come to her. She did not want Amy to feel pushed out by the new baby either. Suzy and Jay had been very careful to include her in plans for the new arrival, and had told her how important it was to be a big sister. Amy rushed to her mother.

Suzy cuddled her little daughter close to her and kissed her. She admired Amy's new baby doll and told Amy how pretty her new baby was.

Suzy's mum and dad had been looking after Amy whilst Suzy was at the hospital. Suzy beamed at her parents, still with her arms around Amy. "Well, what do you think of your new grandson?" she said proudly. Before they could answer, she added " Aren't we clever, we've got one of each now a beautiful perfect family! Mum, Dad, Rob and Amy, I want

4

you to say hello to Bobby Jay Oakland."

Bob Pond's eyes filled with tears. His wife Joycie openly cried. Her tears of joy coursed down her cheek and she did not even bother wiping them away. They both adored their daughter Suzy. They were so happy that she had at last found happiness. It seemed another lifetime away that she was involved with the despicable Billy Jameson. He had been a gambler and had become involved with a loan shark to fund his habit. Poor Suzy had not known any of this. Billy had left Suzy when she was pregnant and had stolen her money. He had gone on to rob his friend Jonny Mason's house. Even worse, when Jonny's father had come home and interrupted the burglary, Billy had stabbed him and left him for dead. It had taken two years for him to be captured. He had always denied being the father of Suzy's little girl. Billy had never adjusted to life behind bars. He had committed suicide while in prison. Poor Suzy had found it all very hard, but she had coped brilliantly, and Bob and Joycie could not be more proud of her. Especially after the terrible tragedy had happened.

Suzy had given birth to a daughter, Ellie May. Ellie May had been born with Down syndrome. It had been a shock at first but she had been the apple of Suzy's eye. She tragically died after running into the road when she heard the ice cream van. Suzy had tried so hard to catch her when she ran off, and was still haunted by guilt at not being able to save her beloved little girl. Ellie May had just started school when the tragedy occurred. It had been a pleasant Saturday in September and Suzy had gone to the park with Ellie May and Suzy's best friend Sarah. For a while, Bob and Joycie Pond wondered if Suzy would ever recover from her loss. She had been so eaten up with guilt and grief. Suzy had managed to get her life back on course though. It had taken a lot of courage to rebuild her life, but she had managed it.

Jay Oakland had been Ellie May's teacher. When Jay and Suzy began to date a year after Ellie May's death, Suzy's parents at last began to see their happy go lucky daughter begin to return. It had taken time but here she was happily married and now with two beautiful children. Jay had been so good for Suzy. Bob and Joycie adored their son in law. He was a wonderful husband and father to little Amy.

"Well Amy, what do you think of your baby brother then?" Bob Pond asked his five year old granddaughter. Amy Oakland leaned over and took a good look at the sleeping baby in her mums' arms.

"He's alright," she declared honestly, shrugging her shoulders. "I'd rather have a puppy though."

ONE YEAR LATER

1988

Louise Bingley- Warrington looked out of the master bedroom window onto the landscaped gardens below. She could just see her husband Rupert over by the hedgerow. He was happily digging. They paid gardeners to take care of the grounds of their large estate but Rupert loved to be hands on when he got the time. He enjoyed getting his hands dirty, he would say. He loved any excuse to pull on his Hunter wellies and waxed jacket and get stuck in. It was his way of relaxing after a hard week at work. He was a barrister and it was not often that he got the opportunity to tend his beloved gardens. Louise sighed. If only such simple pleasures could make her happy. She had really tried to settle down. Rupert adored her and she had everything money could buy. In the five years since they had married they had travelled the world and Rupert had bought her jewellery from Tiffany's and clothes from designers in Paris and Milan. She had her own walk in wardrobe filled with handmade shoes, and handbags that cost enough to make most people's eyes water. Rupert had been hinting about making their happiness complete by starting a family. That had filled Louise with utter panic. Children had never been part of the plan. Not as far as Louise was concerned, anyway. She had never been particularly maternal. The idea of a bunch of mini Rupert's squalling about the place filled her with horror. No, she had decided firmly, it must never happen. Rupert had so far been patient. Louise was, after all, still very young. Rupert was already in his thirties and was keen to become a father. Louise wondered how long it would be before he became impatient with her and started pressurising her. She felt totally stifled as it was. She watched as Rupert filled a wheelbarrow with garden debris and wheeled it across the carefully manicured lawn. She wondered sadly to herself why she could not love her husband. He was reasonably good looking. He had a full head of dark blonde hair and perfect teeth, and a finely honed body. He looked every inch the romantic hero of all the soppy Mills and Boon love stories her mother had always enjoyed reading. He worked out in their home gym regularly and used their swimming pool every morning. He was fabulously wealthy and extremely intelligent. He was attentive, loving and even quite accomplished in bed. All her friends envied her. She had a life style that most people could not even dream of or aspire to. Their house had six bedrooms and extensive grounds. She had it all. Except Jonny Mason.

Louise had been in love with Jonny Mason since she was a school girl. Her father, Gregg Green was an antique dealer and was a business associate of Victor Mason, Jonny's father. Louise liked to tag along with her father when she was bored during school holidays. As soon as she had spotted Jonny on Victor Mason's antique stall one cold December morning, she was smitten. He was unbelievably handsome. He made Rupert seem ordinary looking in comparison. As she watched him smiling at a customer, her heart had done somersaults. He was not just handsome though. He had..what was it? A certain magic about him. He was effortlessly charming he was just so cool. She was obsessed with him. She had tried every trick in the book to get him to love her back. Unfortunately, he had not reciprocated her feelings. He had come to loathe Louise Blakely Green. He had met and married his red haired girlfriend Sarah Miller and broken her heart. Louise found her face growing red as she remembered the desperate measures she had resorted to, in order to try to gain Jonny's attention. She had stolen his house keys once at a party. She had used them to go to his house hoping to find him alone. Louise had been over joyed when Victor Mason had bought a house in Islington. Louise had gone to the City of London School for girls in Islington and it was easy to hop on a bus from her school in the Barbican and walk past the new house in Duncan terrace. She would pretend to be browsing round the shops in Camden Passage to try and get a glimpse of her beloved Jonny. She would often drag her long suffering friend Camilla along so she could pretend to be shopping. They would stop off for coffee and cake in The Dome Café. The café looked out onto Upper Street, right opposite the Business Design Centre. It was on the corner near Camden Passage. Louise would stare out of the window hoping to catch a glimpse of Jonny. Victor had rented a shop there and set up a business that he and Jonny ran together. Jonny shared the new house in Duncan Terrace with his father Victor. The house had been empty when Louise decided to pay Jonny an unexpected visit. She had used the stolen set of keys to let herself in to the house. She had slipped upstairs to Jonny's self-contained flat to wait for him. When Jonny had come home, he had found Louise naked in his bed. Louise had been mortified when she realised Jonny had his girlfriend Sarah with him. That scenario had never occurred to Louise. It had all been horribly embarrassing. Louise wanted the ground to open and swallow her up even now. Especially remembering that even after that hideous episode, she had posted Jonny topless photographs of herself, still hoping in vain to gain his attention. It had all ended badly and her father had insisted that she stay away from Jonny and his entire family. Her mother, Marissa, had been appalled at her daughter's behaviour. Marissa Blakely had been a staunch member of the golf club and had to listen to the club member's gossip about her wayward daughters antics. She had not been amused. Louise had been packed off to University as far away from London as possible. She had met Rupert at a party held by one of her new university chums. Rupert had been a rich uncle of Chloe, Louise's classmate. Egged on by Chloe, Louise, rather drunk at the time, had flirted like mad with Rupert. Rupert had been surprised and flattered by a young attractive woman's attention. Louise knew how to turn on the charm when she wanted to. She also knew which buttons to press in the bedroom. She had   practised on many young men on her college campus. She had felt incredibly lonely being so far away from Jonny and had hoped that sex with virtual strangers would be a comfort. It had not, of course. She had decided to concentrate her energies on her studies instead she tried hard to focus, but her heart was never really in it. Then she had met Rupert in her final year and the whole charade had begun again. She had revelled in the attention at first. Rupert had thought she was as much in love with him as he was with her. Six months after their first date at her graduation ceremony, Rupert had proposed. Like a fool, she had accepted his proposal. Now here she was, trapped.

Louise decided that it was about time she went on a shopping spree to London. She badly needed to escape. She would stay in her parents' Pie de Terre in the Barbican. She would not tell anyone that she would also look in on Jonny Mason. She felt that enough water had passed under the bridge now to look up her old friend again. Surely, it was time to let bygones be bygones and start afresh. This time she would take a softly softly approach. She smiled to herself and went to pack.

Violet Jameson hummed tunelessly as she dusted her living room. Her husband Don tried not to get annoyed as she stood in the way of the television. Not that Violet would notice if he got annoyed. She lived in her own little world these days Don thought sadly. Violet had been recently diagnosed with Alzheimer's. She had been acting oddly for some time and Don had been at a loss to know what to do. Her condition was deteriorating quite rapidly now. Don did not know how long he could manage with her at home. They had moved out of their flat on the Packington Estate once their son Graham had left home permanently. They now had a nice little ground floor flat with a bit of outside space. Don was not much of a gardener, he had never had one before, but he enjoyed pottering about and was experimenting with growing vegetables. He had even been to the library and borrowed as many books on growing veg as he could. The new flat was in Essex Road, not too far from where they used to live. Violet kept forgetting they had moved house. At least once a week Don got a phone call from an old neighbour to tell him that Violet had been trying to get back into their old flat again. Once she had wondered off at three in the morning, still in her nightie. Don had been put in touch with social services to try to get a bit of help with the old girl. They were a useless bunch of tossers though, he thought scathingly. They had come round with their clipboards and done all sorts of tests and assessments. They asked Violet endless stupid questions like what year was it and who the bloody prime minister was. Violet had looked at them patiently and spoken to them as if speaking to a child. Of course, she had answered all their questions and been spot on. That didn't mean a thing, Don told them desperately. "Try asking her who I am!" he had said angrily to the young woman sitting on his couch with her hippy shawl and curly hair. "Some days she doesn't know me from Adam!" he had shouted at her. "She gets up at two in the morning and cooks breakfast, thinking it's morning" Don told the latest woman with a clipboard, a note of desperation creeping into his voice. He was having trouble sleeping with all the stress and it was frustrating having to explain how hard it was to a woman young enough to be his daughter. He knew in his heart they were trying their best to help, but he was becoming more and more frustrated. "Sometimes she wants to go off shopping in her nightdress at ten at night. She can tell you what she had for dinner thirty years ago, but can't remember that her eldest son is dead, or remember what his name is. Most of the time she thinks I'm her dad. It's downright dangerous love. Yesterday she left the gas on. I'm at me wits end with her now." The earnest young woman wrote notes and nodded sympathetically. Don gritted his teeth as he saw her out and slammed the door shut behind her. She looked like yet another useless one. All sympathetic smiles and no action. He wondered how much longer he would be expected to cope alone. He had married for better or worse but nothing had prepared him for what he was going through now.

Sarah Mason kissed her little daughter Lydia and pulled the bedcovers up to make her comfortable. "Goodnight sweetheart, sweet dreams. Daddy will be in to give you a kiss in a minute. He's just making me a cuppa," she said as she stood up. She put the storybook back on her daughter's bookshelf. "Hmm" she said, feigning innocence, "I hope Shady is not in that bed with you"

Shady was their black Labrador. Sarah could clearly see her rudder like tail thumping happily from under her daughter's bed covers. Lydia giggled. "Oh no mum, Shady's not in here." Sarah smiled. They had the same conversation every bedtime. "That's all right then" she said and quietly left the room. She could hear Lydia giggling and talking to Shady under the covers as she headed for the sofa. Sarah smiled as she heard the familiar sounds. She wanted to have a chat with her husband Jonny though. She had something on her mind.

"Ooh thanks, Jon" Sarah said gratefully as she saw the steaming mug of tea on the table. "Don't be too long with Lyddy tonight. I want to tell you something."

Sarah sipped her tea as she curled up on the sofa and smiled as she listened to the giggling coming from her daughter's bedroom. Jonny, she knew, would be in there for a while. He adored his daughter and bedtime was always special. He would tell her a story, about Miss Silly Sausage and her doggy detective Missy Mustard, then he would put on a silly Shady the dog voice and there would always be much giggling and lots of laughter. Sarah did not mind waiting. Jonny was a wonderful father. So different from her own, she thought wistfully. She sipped her tea again and quickly tried to think of happier things. She did not like to remember her own brutal father. He was dead and Sarah had to remind herself every day that he could not hurt her or her beloved mum Carrie any more. Bedtime had always been a tense time for her growing up. Many a night she had lain in her bed, hearing her mother screaming through the thin dividing wall as her father Tommy used his fists again. Sarah would lie, quietly sobbing, with her pillow over her head to try to drown out the sound. She knew from bitter experience that if she ran in to try to help it would only make things worse. Her father would simply beat her mother even more for the interference. Every day had been filled with fear for her and her mother. Tommy had been a volatile bomb of a man, just waiting to explode. Sarah drank her tea and tried to erase the dark cloud that still haunted her every day.

 Eventually Shady came lolloping out of the bedroom followed by Jonny. He smiled sheepishly. "Sorry, I got carried away. That Missy Mustard was hot stuff tonight." He winked at Sarah and she groaned at his feeble joke. "Budge up, hun. What do you want to tell me?"

"Well, Suzy and Jay have invited us for dinner tomorrow. Suzy has a great idea she wants to discuss. We've talked about it together, and we want to know what you think."
"Oh, that sounds dangerous" Jon said, grinning. He was very fond of Sarah's friend. He admired her courage and she had always been loyal to Sarah. "Why don't we go to Fredericks? I fancy a good night out. Give Suze a ring and tell her I'm paying."

Fredericks was a very posh and very expensive restaurant in Camden Passage. The food was wonderful, but the prices made Suzy's eyes water. She had never lived down the embarrassing time when she had gone there with Jay shortly after they first got together. She had picked Fredericks hoping to impress Jay. She had insisted on paying her own way when she had seen the prices on the menu though. She had not wanted Jay to think she was the gold digging type. She had been very impressed with Jay when he had flatly refused to take her money. She had never been inside Fredericks but had passed it on numerous occasions and thought it looked marvellous. A very snooty waiter had showed them to a table and had brought a bowl of crudités over when

13

she had been on her date with Jay. Suzy had never had these before. There were carrot and cucumber batons arranged beautifully in a glass bowl. Radishes had been carved into flowers and were arranged around the edge of the bowl. It looked like a work of art. Next to the veg sticks was another little bowl with some creamy white stuff in it. Suzy happily dunked her carrot sticks into it, thinking it was a dip for the crudités. Jay had done the same. It was not until the waiter brought rolls to the table that Suzy realised they had eaten the butter. The waiter had looked appalled when Suzy had politely asked for butter for the rolls, and had said cuttingly "Madam has already eaten it". Jay had laughed until his eyes watered and Suzy knew in that moment that she loved him with all her heart. They had not been back to Fredericks since. She hoped old snooty had forgotten her by now.

Jonny Mason knew the Maître De, Pierre, at Fredericks. Jon and his father Victor had an antique shop in Camden Passage. They specialised in antique toys. Their shop was only a few feet away from the restaurant. Pierre Gamonia collected lead soldiers and often popped into their shop for a chat. Jon had teased him for having such a clichéd French name. Pierre had been a good sport and had laughed too. He was a good customer. He in return had said to Jonny in his deep French accent, "What about your name? they call you Jonny? What are you, a giant condom?" They had laughed together. Jonny called him Mr Cliché and Pierre called Jonny Mr Condom. It was always good to exchange a bit of banter with customers. Jonny would look out for anything he thought Pierre would be interested in when he was at auctions or antique fairs.

Pierre welcomed them in and showed them to their table. He winked at Jonny and hissed in a stage whisper "The best table for Mr Condom and his friends"

Suzy looked around shiftily but was relieved that there was no sign of the snooty waiter from her previous visit. As if reading her mind Jay said, "No dunking your carrot sticks in the butter tonight, Suze." He grinned at her as she hid her head in the large menu.

"Oh don't!" she replied, peering shiftily over the top. "I hope he ain't here tonight. It was a good few years ago. Maybe he's left now. "

"I'd have loved to have been here. " Sarah said, giggling. Suzy had told Sarah and Jonny all about it.

"Well in my defence, it didn't look like butter. It was pale and definitely not what I buy at home. I'm sticking to my Anchor butter. Anyway, I can't wait any longer. I'm bursting to tell you my plan!"

The waiter appeared at that moment to take their order. When he had finished writing everything down Suzy continued. "Jon, what do you think of me and Sarah starting up our own business? "

Jon raised his eyebrows in surprise, but said "Go on, I'm all ears."

Suzy and Sarah had worked together in Debenhams department store since they were sixteen. They had worked in the gift-wrapping department. Suzy had been on maternity leave with Bobby Jay and been absolutely devastated when their boss Mr Michaelson had called her and told her sadly that he was retiring and the gift wrapping department was being discontinued. There was no longer a job for her to go back to once her maternity leave was over. Sarah had also been distraught at the news. Their floor manager, Miss Parish had always been supportive and had tried her best to find them jobs elsewhere in the store. The only thing available had been full time in separate departments. One vacancy was in the carpet show room and the other position was in the men's underwear section. Their old adversary Pervy Patrick still worked in the men's department. He was still prone to staring at any woman's bosom and still leered at every woman with a pulse. His prominent Adams apple still bobbed up and down in his throat and he still wore his hideous kipper ties. He was not one to move with the current trends and seemed to be stuck in the 1970's groove he so favoured. Unfortunately, he had divorced his poor put upon wife and now he was free and single again he was forever on the prowl for a new woman. The prospect of being on his hit list did not exactly thrill either Sarah or Suzy.

The carpet department was down in the lower ground floor and was staffed exclusively by aging bald men. All they ever seemed to talk about was golf, who was running in the Grand National or how England was doing at cricket. Not exactly hot topics for most women. Not that many women were daft enough to want to disturb their little world. Suzy wondered if they had rolled up any female staff members who had been foolhardy enough to venture into that male domain. Maybe they had gagged them, fearing they would blurt out something about child birth or become menopausal in front of them. She pictured a poor middle-aged woman, having a hot flush, trussed up in the Axminster, and left to rot. There would be no other women to talk to down there and they were hardly ever rushed off their feet. Not even any customers to break the tedium. There was never much of a demand on carpet sales. One could die of boredom down there and probably not be noticed for several months. They would probably sweep her under a rug and leave her there until a customer eventually wandered in and tripped over her. Suzy did not think she would last an hour down there, let alone a whole day. The thought of that or having to endure Pervy Patrick all day every day was purgatory. Sarah had said she would rather eat her own liver and Suzy had nodded grimly in agreement. Reluctantly both Suzy and Sarah had decided to leave Debenhams. They had a tearful leaving party. Even the horrible Pan Stick people from the makeup counters had come along and wished them well. For the past six month's both Suzy and Sarah had been staying at home with the children. It had been fun, but both wanted a bit of independence and a bit more stimulation now that their little girls were at school. Miss Parish had stayed in touch with them both and it had been her suggestion that had made Suzy so excited. Her eyes shone as she spoke. "I've had a word with the market inspector in Chapel market," Suzy said excitedly as they all tucked into their starters. "He is a nice bloke called Adam Sandford. Anyway, I asked him about a stall. It was Miss Parish's idea. She said why didn't me and Sarah start our own gift wrap and card shop? We could do cards, wrapping paper, gift baskets... we could offer a gift wrapping service too, like we had in Debenhams. I'm sure we could make a go of it. Anyway, the market inspector said there wasn't a stall going, but there is a shop unit that's empty. There is usually a waiting list for the shops, but the other possible traders that have applied for it are not suitable. The inspector said he wanted something original. He liked our idea of themed gift baskets as well as gift-wrapping and high quality greeting cards. There are too many clothes shops and food shops down the market already. Well, if we want it, and we can come up with the money to rent it, it's ours!"

Jonny looked at Suzy and Sarah's excited faces. He looked at Jay. Jay had been so good for Suzy. Jonny still felt guilty for introducing her to his erstwhile friend Billy Jameson. Billy had deceived all of them. Jonny had never got over the betrayal. Especially as his father still bore the scars where Billy had stabbed him. Billy had never accepted that he had been the father of Suzy's daughter Ellie May, either. He really had been a spiteful twisted excuse for a human being. Poor Suzy had not told Billy about her pregnancy. It had been Billy's mother, Violet, who had told him that he was the father. Ellie May had been a beautiful child. Jonny and Sarah had both adored her. Billy's mother Violet had been disgusted with her son. She had shown Billy a photograph of his daughter when she visited him in prison. He had said scathingly that he could not have fathered a mongol child like that. Violet had stopped

17

visiting her son after that vile remark. She could not forgive him for all the terrible things he had done. She had grown very fond of her granddaughter. However, she had unfortunately blamed Suzy for Ellie May's death and they had since lost contact now.

Jonny had been heart broken when Ellie May had died in that tragic accident. His beautiful Sarah had been with them on the day it happened. He had held her in his arms many a night after the terrible tragedy as she sobbed out her grief. He really admired the way Suzy had pulled her life back together. He would do anything he could to help her and his beloved Sarah. He knew that they would do well. He raised his glass and said, "Here's to you two then. You know I'll do all I can to help. When do we get started?"

CHAPTER TWO

Sarah was teetering on the top rung of a stepladder arranging stock on the shelves of the new shop. It had all gone much better than they had expected. Everyone had pitched in to help and she and Suzy were very grateful. Victor had put them in touch with a company he had dealt with who supplied shop fittings. Suzy's younger brother Robert had helped redecorate and customise the interior. He had also agreed to be their delivery driver. The shop had been open for six months and the themed gift baskets had proved to be extremely popular. Especially when Suzy had a brain wave and they had offered the home delivery service. Now they were preparing for the Christmas rush. Miss Parish had once again been a star and had given them the name of an amazing window dresser friend of hers. As a favour to Eleanor Parish, she had done a fabulous eye-catching window display for the shop. It was a real showstopper. She had transformed their window into a miniature Santa's workshop, complete with elves, and had included as many items sold in the shop as she could. There was a beautifully decorated little Christmas tree, complete with lights, and lots of glittery snow. All the children for miles around had come to look at the display. It was truly magical. Amy and Lydia loved it. They had stood outside in the cold staring at it until Suzy and Sarah had insisted they come in and get warm. Sarah had made them all mugs of hot chocolate to thaw out.

Penny Chalmers, the window dresser was newly retired and told Sarah and Suzy cheerfully that she was happy to help any time. Over her third cup of coffee, she admitted that she was bored stupid rattling around in her flat with too much time on her hands. She had loads of ideas for other themes for the window and had lots of props she said they could use. "They are only gathering dust in my work room now dears," she had said a little wistfully. "Just let me know what you want for the New Year, and I'll bring it along. If that brother of yours could pick me up and save me having to carry it all here, I'll be more than happy to help."

Suzy and Sarah's mums helped out with baby sitting and Marlayna, Victor Masons partner helped in the shop when needed. The girls had a steady flow of customers most days. They still did their gift-wrapping and at this time of year, it was extremely popular. They had a counter set up especially for gift-wrapping demonstrations and it drew quite a crowd. It had taken some getting used to not having a boss breathing down their necks. "You know, I actually miss the Pan Stick people!" Suzy said to Sarah. Sarah slowly came down from the stepladder. She could not reach the top shelves without it. "I know what you mean. It's odd not having them glaring over at us all day. We've got no one to wind up either, have we? I miss that. I wonder how pervy Patrick is? I bet he's been lusting after some poor girl. Ooh, Suze, turn the radio up! Remember this?"

Suzy was sitting behind the counter. She leant behind her where the radio sat nestled on its shelf. They liked to have it playing quietly in the background. "Rock the boat" was playing. This had been one of their favourite songs when they used to go to the Lyceum as teenage girls. It brought back such happy memories. The two of them had practised their dance steps for hours in front of their bedroom mirrors to get their dance moves perfect for their nights out. There were no customers in the shop at the moment, so both girls made the most of the lull in trade and began singing along. Sarah started dancing and Suzy of course joined in. "Rock the boat..don't tip the boat over.." they sang at the top of their voices. Sarah began dancing up and down the shop, swaying amongst the greeting cards.

"Er...yoohoo ladies, am I interrupting the party?" a male voice said loudly above the noise. Adam Sandford the market inspector stood in the doorway. "Woops!" said Suzy, laughing. "No, come in, I'll put the kettle on"

  Adam Sandford had become very fond of the two bright young women who had recently rented the shop in Chapel Market. He was particularly fond of the beautiful Sarah Mason. It was such a shame she was married. Her husband was a nice bloke, too. Mores the pity, he thought. No chance of nipping in and stealing her away from him, he thought sadly. Sarah was obviously head over heels in love with her husband, even a blind man could spot it. Her face lit up like Blackpool illuminations every time she mentioned his name. Just as well, really, Adam mused. He could do without the hassle that women brought. Adam was divorced and had not been looking for a commitment again. He had steered clear of any female company until he had met the delectable Mrs Mason. Sarah had reawakened his spirits somewhat. He was content to lust from afar for now. It had been a particularly messy divorce and he had needed time to recover. He felt it wise to avoid any further complications until he had sorted his head out. He could not seem to stay away from the pretty little shop or its glamorous sales assistants though. He liked the shop name, Bow Diddly. It made him smile, and he loved the eye catching displays. At the moment it was spectacular, and had been drawing crowds. He was always pleased when any of his traders attracted new business. The shop had been good for business on the stalls in the market too. The two young women had proved to have good business heads. There had been a lot of resentment at first amongst the stallholders. There was a waiting list for the shop units. Adam had not been too popular when he had first authorised the shop to newcomers. Some felt that they had served their time out in all weathers and deserved a nice warm shop unit. However, even the stallholders had had to grudgingly admit it had been a wise move. The girls had been like a breath of fresh air. They had done a great job of advertising in the local Gazette and in the very trendy Camden Passage. They had given out little favours of sweets on their opening day and free balloons. The girls had dressed up, and taken it in turns to wander up and down the market handing out free goodies to all the passers-by. They had been well received. Their eye catching delivery van was now a familiar site in the area. Adam had laughingly taken one of their free chocolates on opening day and loved the tea and coffee that they had given to their customers. He told them that he was always open to bribery so long as they provided a nice cup of tea. They always put the kettle on for him and he dropped by most days for elevenses. They took it in turns to do the cake run and had a nice bit of banter. It made his days a lot more pleasant and took his mind of off some of the grumpy stallholders he had to pacify and his lying, cheating ex-wife and her body-building boyfriend.

"Is that kettle on?" Adam inquired, joining in with the dancing and doing an impressive John Travolta impression. "Coming up" said Sarah, sashaying along the shop floor towards their little back room. "I got you a custard slice. Is that okay?" she called to Adam as she filled the kettle. "Lovely" he said, leaning on the counter beside Suzy. Sarah appeared shortly carrying two steaming mugs. Suzy and Adam took theirs gratefully and Sarah nipped back for her own mug and the box of cakes. Sarah perched on her stall behind the counter and took a bite out of her London cheesecake. She delicately picked a strand of coconut from her chin and popped it into her mouth. Adam tried not to stare. Oh Lord, she is gorgeous he told himself.

Suzy had a chocolate éclair. She licked the cream silently and observed the way Adam looked at her best friend. We will have to keep our eye on that one she told herself.

Jay Oakland knocked on the new head teacher's office door and waited to be summoned inside. Sheila Knight had only been appointed in

September. Jay was still undecided whether he liked her or not. She was pleasant enough and she certainly had the children's best interests at heart. So far, she had failed to make much of an impact on Jay. He had the greatest respect for her predecessor, Margaret Saunders. He had been devastated when she had told the staff quietly that her father had suffered a stroke. She told them sadly she would be leaving the position she had held for the past twenty years to go and nurse him in her old family home in Devon. Jay missed her. She had been a gifted teacher and an inspiring head.

Jay entered the room when he heard Sheila Knight call a curt "Come!"

"Ah, Jay. What can I do for you? Please, take a seat" Sheila Knight said. Jay sat in the chair opposite her desk. He launched straight in. "I'm worried about a pupil in my class, Sheila, Dennis Crayford. He seems to have a lot of bruises on a regular basis. I have mentioned it to his mum and she says he gets them from his seizures. I'm not so sure though. They don't seem consistent to me with bruises from bumping himself when he has seizures. To be honest, his new stepfather seems like a nasty sort. Dennis never seemed to be bruised like that before he came along, and he had plenty of seizures last term. Nothing specific yet but…" Jay's voice trailed off as he watched the expression on the new heads face. He had seen that dismissive look so many times before. He clenched his fists and tried to remain calm. Sheila Knight raised her eyebrows. Martin Crayford, Dennis' stepfather had always seemed perfectly pleasant to her. She looked concerned but said, "We have to tread carefully here. Just because you don't like the look of him does not mean he is being abusive. We can't throw accusations around until we are certain. " Jay felt himself bristle. He was sick and tired of the politically correct brigade. Dennis Crayford was a vulnerable young lad. He had mild learning difficulties and severe epilepsy. His mother, Adele, was a single parent until recently. Her new husband often came to collect Dennis since the wedding in the summer holidays and Jay did not

23

like his attitude towards the child when Adele was not around. Poor Dennis seemed terrified of him. He had been a happy little boy and had been doing well in class until his mother had remarried. Now he was withdrawn and always looked so sad. He knew that look meant something was very wrong at home. He had seen that same expression on his own face many years ago and he wanted so much to erase it from his mind. It brought back too many memories of his own troubled childhood.

Jay had grown up in a children's home. He had been taken in to care at the age of seven when his own parents had been killed in a car crash. He had been on a sleep over at his friend's house when the accident happened. All his family had been wiped out on that terrible night. He had never quite come to terms with the guilt of being the only survivor.it had been difficult for a young boy to understand how his mum and dad could be there one day and gone the next. He had been angry with them. How could they leave him? He had needed them so much. He was full of fear. Who would look after him now? He had been driven to the local children's home. All the staff had been very kind to him, but it had felt at first like being in hospital. They had cared because they were paid to do so, it was their job. They had tried their best. He had several foster families over the years. Some had been fine, some had been horrible one had been a nightmare. None had cared enough to adopt him. He had wondered during the lonely nights at the children's home why no long lost relatives had ever come to claim him. Surely, he must have had an auntie or an uncle who wanted him. He always seemed to find himself back in the care home after a few short months with foster carers. He bounced from one disaster to another. He had become increasingly disruptive as he was passed like a parcel from one family to another. He would have gone seriously off the rails if it had not been for his form teacher, Mr Mathews. He had become involved with a gang of boys by the time he was twelve who hanged around the streets smoking, glue sniffing, drinking, and bunking off school. They robbed houses and broke into cars. For a while, Jay had not cared what happened to him. The gang admired him, for he appeared fearless. He did not have to do much to impress them. He already had a reputation. His couldn't care less attitude got him noticed by the gang leader. No one cared about him, so why should he care? He was accepted for the first time since his parents had been killed. He began getting into all sorts of trouble. The more outlandish the plan, the more attention he got from the other members. It had felt like he had a family at last. The care home were deeply concerned about his antics and had to intervene. They were receiving more and more calls from the police regarding young Jay Oakland. He had been moved to a new children's home, far away from the gang members. He went to a new secondary school in Islington. He had not liked that idea one bit, but it had been his salvation.

James Mathews had nurtured the bright fragile boy he had seen during Jay's first term in his class at   secondary school. He had slowly gained Jay's trust and it had been he that inspired Jay to take up teaching as a career. No one had ever encouraged him before or believed in him. Mr Matthews had not only encouraged him but had provided a listening ear all through his school days. He had recognised that he was a bright boy, and without Jay even realising at first he had steered him into making the right decisions about his future. Jay shuddered to think what might have become of him if he had not had someone like Mr Mathews. Jay had made some good friends at his school too. Friends who realised there was more to life than wasting time drinking and smoking on street corners and getting into petty crime. He had managed to avoid trouble and had stayed in touch with James Mathews long after he left school. He had been devastated when he had died of a heart attack shortly after retiring from teaching. His legacy had never left him though and he would always cherish his memories. He tried not to dwell on his past before he was taken under Mr Mathews' wing. It was too painful. He considered himself a very lucky man these days. He had his beautiful Suzy and his lovely little family. Boys like Dennis Crayford brought it all back, though. He sometimes still had nightmares about his time with the Robertson's. Barry Robertson had told him he would find him if he ever told. Jay never did tell. He had been a frightened little boy caught up in a nightmare, where all the grownups he had ever trusted had been cruelly snatched away. They had been replaced with ones who never listened, and were out to get him. He bore the scars and kept the silence even now. Suzy did not know the full story of what had happened to him back then. It was too painful to put into words. Jay could spot a sadist a mile off though. He had a gut feeling about Martin bloody Crayford. It made him sick to the stomach. He reminded him too much of Barry Robertson. He had the same smarminess, the same deceitful look in his eye. He might have so far managed to pull the wool over Sheila's eyes, but Jay saw right through him. He would not allow any other child to suffer as he had done all those long lonely years ago. He saw the same fears in Dennis Crayford's eyes that he had seen in his own eyes when he had been at the mercy of Barry "It's for your own good son" Robertson.

Sheila Knight could see how concerned Jay Oakland was. Although she had not been at Bonny Ridge School very long she had been assured that Jay was a rare breed. Margaret Saunders, her predecessor had described him as unique. She had been advised by the former head to trust his judgement. She had observed him in the classroom and he was obviously passionate about his work. All his pupils seemed to adore him and he was well respected by all the other members of staff. She promised to keep monitoring the situation and asked Jay to report back to her if he had any further concerns. She handed over a form. "I will speak to the school welfare officer. Make sure your concerns are well documented, and I will pass your concerns on to her. Please keep me posted. " she added. She waved her hand towards the door signalling that the discussion was over. Jay stood up to leave, still with his fists tightly clenched and his jaw set. He'd keep her informed alright. From now on, he would be watching Martin Crayford like a bloody hawk.

Suzy came back from the morning cake run clearly upset. "What's up?" Sarah said, concerned. She handed Suzy a tissue. Suzy had tears in her eyes. "I've just seen Violet." Suzy said, blowing her nose.

"Violet? What, Billy's mum, Violet?" Sarah said incredulously. Suzy nodded. "What did that old cow want?"

Sarah had never forgiven Violet Jameson for how she treated Suzy when Ellie May died. Suzy had been devastated at the loss of her child and wracked with guilt. She blamed herself even though it had been a tragic accident. Ellie May had let go of Suzy's hand on that fateful day, and shot across the park like a firework. Both Suzy and Sarah had chased after her, screaming her name to come back, but it had been too late. Violet had not helped by accusing Suzy of neglect. It had almost destroyed poor Suzy. She still had nightmares about it. Jay often had to hold her and sooth her in the night when she awoke screaming for her lost little girl. Her dreams were always the same. She would be running in slow motion and never able to catch up with Ellie May. She would relive that terrible scene over and over again. Her child, her precious baby, lying broken and bloody in the road outside of the park.

"It was very odd. I don't think she's all there. She greeted me like a long lost friend." Suzy's eyes filled with fresh tears. "She...she asked me how Ellie May was."

CHAPTER THREE

Carrie Miller hummed along to the radio as she rolled out pastry. She was making sausage rolls for her beautiful granddaughter Lydia. Her sausage rolls were Lydia's favourite and she was coming for tea today after school. Carrie did not make sausage rolls very often these days but thought she would treat Lydia today. It was only a couple of weeks until Christmas and she was making a big batch to pop into the freezer. She liked to plan ahead. She had been feeding her Christmas cakes with brandy since October, and she already had four dozen mince pies in her faithful old freezer. She made plenty to share and always made Christmas cakes for Suzy and Joycie. She enjoyed decorating the finished iced cakes and choosing different designs every year. She also had a huge Christmas pudding that was covered in a muslin cloth waiting to be steamed on the big day. There were smaller covered puddings set aside for Suzy and Jay and for Joycie and Bob too. Carrie enjoyed making up little food hampers every year for those she loved. She filled her hampers with all the homemade goodies she baked. Each year the wicker baskets would be returned empty in January, ready to fill again for the next Christmas. They were always very well received. She had hidden old fashioned silver sixpences inside the Christmas pudding she would share with the family on the big day. She always did this for Lydia to find, carefully wrapped in grease proof paper. Lydia loved this tradition. She knew that Jonny and Sarah would watch carefully in case Lydia choked, just as she had done long ago with Sarah when she was small. They would secretly make sure that Lydia found most of the sixpences, to bring her good luck for the New Year. Whoever found the most sixpences would get the best luck. It was an added bit of Christmas magic that Carrie loved. She pictured Lydia's delighted little face as she found the secret sixpences on her plate and smiled to herself. It was a far cry from the bad old days. One year her husband Tommy had accidently got a sixpence in his serving of pudding. He had nearly choked on it, and Carrie had rushed to fetch him a glass of water. He had been fine but he had told Carrie she was a stupid bitch, and had slapped her hard across the face. She had fallen, knocking the remains of her carefully prepared Christmas dinner to the ground. Poor Sarah had screamed, which had only enraged Tommy even more. He pulled Carrie up by her hair and punched her. Carrie closed her eyes and tried to erase the dark dreadful memories. Maybe that was why she was always a bit anxious about Little Lydia choking. She tried to remain calm, but she knew Sarah understood. She always gave Carrie a reassuring pat on the hand as the pudding was served on the big day. It did not do to dwell on the past. Carrie wiped her hands on her apron and smiled to herself. It was all over now, and Christmas was a happy time again. She put the radio on and hummed tunelessly as she busied herself in her little kitchen.

Carrie had not been feeling well lately. She wanted to get the sausage rolls in the oven, and go and have a sit down and a cuppa. She had been getting some worrying chest pains again. They had been getting worse in recent weeks. She could feel the familiar tightening of her chest beginning again as she wiped flour off her kitchen counter. She wondered if she should make another appointment and see the doctor. She had put it off, as she was so busy getting ready for Christmas. Her GP had diagnosed her with angina, and she had some pills to take. She also had a spray she was meant to use. She had to spray it under her tongue if she had pain. She stopped what she was doing for a moment and obediently used the spray. She kept it in her apron pocket. She had not told Sarah, she did not want to worry her. The medication did not seem to be doing much good. The pains were becoming more frequent. Maybe they were panic attacks. The memories of Tommy always made her feel bad. She had seen a programme on television about panic attacks. Perhaps it was nothing serious. She still volunteered and did her job at the women's refuge but she had cut her hours down. She only went in one day a week now. Even that was getting a bit much. She did not like to admit it, but she felt like she was getting old. She was worrying about how to tell them at the refuge that she could not manage any more. Now that Sarah was running her own business with Suzy, Carrie was needed more at home anyway. Carrie helped out by picking up Lydia from school and looking after her until Sarah or Jonny finished work. She loved it, she felt good being useful, but looking after a lively six year old was sometimes exhausting. Carrie had also been busy with her Christmas shopping. She had almost finished now. She hoped that Lydia would like the presents she had bought for her. She had bought Lydia a dolls house and lots of furniture to go inside it. She could not wait to see her darling little face on Christmas morning when she opened all the parcels from Father Christmas. Carrie had knitted Lydia a stocking to hang up when she had been a baby. Lydia still used it and hung it on her bedpost every year. She decided to get Christmas out of the way before going back to her GP. The surgery in Bath Street was busy at the best of times. She could not face having to sit in the waiting room for hours when she had so much to do. No, she told herself resolutely, let's get Christmas over and then she would go and see the doctor again if the pain got any worse.

Carrie was very grateful that Sarah and Jonny always insisted she stay with them at Christmas. It was wonderful to wake up to a house filled with noise and happy laughter. Victor Mason and his lovely partner Marlayna lived in the downstairs part of the house in Duncan Terrace and Sarah, Jonny and Lydia lived in the flat above. They had had a loft extension when Lydia was born to give them some extra space. Carrie slept down stairs though when she went to stay, in Victor's spare room and he and Marlayna always made her so welcome. She was really looking forward to it. Since becoming a widow, she had become used to the quiet of her little flat, but Christmas time was horrible for the lonely.

Carrie felt very blessed to have family and good friends around whenever she needed company. Christmas had always been a particularly stressful time when her husband Tommy had been alive. He had drunk even more then. Her nerves had always jangled, trying to keep him happy. There had been many years when all she had for Christmas were bruises and broken bones. The sixpence incidence was just one in a long line of horror stories that she would rather forget. She shuddered, and told herself again not to dwell on the past. He was dead and buried and could not hurt her any more. Now it would be filled with laughter. She could not wait.

"Dennis, come on, love. You know I have to go to work. Daddy will get your dinner for you. I'll be home before you know it."

"He's not my Daddy!" Dennis said sulkily, lying on the carpet and howling loudly. Adele Crayford sighed impatiently. She did not have time for any more of her son's tantrums. She was already in trouble at work for being late twice last week. She could not afford another blot on her copy book. Her evening cleaning job helped to tide them over and provided some nice treats for Dennis. It had been bloody hard managing on her own, especially with a kid like Dennis. He had been brain damaged during a difficult birth when he had become starved of oxygen. The traumatic birth had almost killed them both. He had been diagnosed with developmental delay in his pre-school days. They had told her at the baby clinic that Dennis had not met his developmental targets, whatever that meant. She knew he had been slow to crawl and walk, or even sit up. He had got there in the end though. Adele had not been overly concerned until the nurse had mentioned it. He had been such a good baby. She had held him in her arms at the hospital and had named him after her own father. She missed her dad very much. He had been a scaffolder and had died after a fall on a building site. Adele had only been seven years old at the time.
 She had never had any dealings with little babies before, and just thought her Dennis was a placid child. Then, the educational welfare people had given him the label of learning difficulties. Without a label,

Dennis would never have qualified for his place at Bonny Ridge, but it had been very difficult to come to terms with. Adele had gone through a period of deep mourning for the healthy baby she thought she had given birth to. Dennis loved his school, though and was very happy, particularly since he had been in Mr Oakland's class. He had started having seizures shortly after his third birthday and had been a handful ever since. Adele was reluctant to admit it but she had found it difficult to cope on her own. It had been a relief when Dennis started school. She had a few hours alone where she did not have to have eyes in the back of her head. Just being able to go and have a nice bath without being interrupted was a luxury. Mr Oakland and the rest of the staff at Bonny Ridge were amazing. Adele's mind was at rest when Dennis was at school. He was in the safest of hands there. Adele had been frantic when Dennis had first started having seizures. It was a huge shock as it slowly dawned on her that she had a child with special needs. He had been in and out of hospital and eventually diagnosed with epilepsy. His medical condition had caused problems between her and his dad, Jimmy. Jimmy had not been able to cope. They had tried to make a go of it when Adele had become pregnant but it had never been easy once the baby arrived. Adele had always been tired and Jimmy had said he felt trapped and tied down. It was not poor little Dennis' fault. Yes, he was a handful, but he could not help it. He was a loving sweet and gentle boy. He sometimes had seizures during the night and often wet the bed. Adele had forgotten what it was like to have an undisturbed night's sleep. Always Adele got up to see to Dennis. Jimmy would pretend to be asleep, the lazy swine. Adele could not help feeling resentful. Dennis was a huge responsibility but he should have been Jimmy's responsibility too. It would have been far easier to cope if the load had been shared. Ha fat chance, Adele thought bitterly. Jimmy had buggered off before Dennis was four. He ran off with a tart he had met at his job in the supermarket. Good bloody riddance Adele had told herself bitterly.

However if life had been hard before, it became a nightmare trying to cope completely alone. She had let her friends fade away and had lost contact with most of them while she struggled to bring up Dennis. He was a loving child, but Adele could not take her eye off him for a second. She worried that he would hurt himself while he was fitting,

32

and he had little sense of danger. It was exhausting. She had no locks on any of the doors at home, in case Dennis accidently locked himself in. It meant that Dennis would barge into the toilet or her bedroom. There was never any privacy, but Adele was used to that now. Well, most of the time she told herself ruefully.

Adele had not thought any man would ever look at her again when Jimmy left. She looked run down and worn out, she could not afford fancy clothes or trips to the hairdresser. Her roots needed doing and the years of sleepless nights and stress were etched on her face. Who would want her, a clapped out penniless woman with a kid who had special needs?

When she had met Martin Crayford, she could not believe her luck. She had been on a rare night out. Her mum had agreed to babysit. Her mum lived in Norfolk and they had never been that close. She did not see her mother very often, but she was the only relative she had, and Adele felt there was simply no one else to turn to. Adele had rung her mum in desperation one day after Dennis had had a particularly bad seizure. Her mum had heard the hysterical note in her daughter's voice and got on the next train. She had come to stay to try to help ease the relationship between them and give her poor frazzled child's nerves time to recuperate. Adele had thought cynically that her mum must have got a touch of guilt and wanted to make amends. Still she had been very grateful and aimed to make the most of it.

Her mum had seen how much Adele needed a break from Dennis the minute she walked in the door. Adele had eagerly taken up her offer to babysit so she could have a rare night off. She had not had a night out in years. She had treated herself to a box of hair dye and spent all afternoon tarting herself up. Finally let off the leash, Adele had called some old pals up and they had gone on a pub crawl.

By the time they had reached The Passage pub in Upper Street, Adele was already well and truly pickled. She was she told herself, woefully out of practise. She had become a lightweight when it came to drinking and had downed several vodka and tonics whilst she caught up with all the gossip and renewed her friendships again. When she had guzzled her third large drink, she was feeling no pain and loved the entire world. She had stopped feeling guilty about pissing her money up the wall.

Booze was hideously expensive on a night out. She tried not to think of how many groceries she could be buying with the cost of a large vodka and tonic. Her mum had given her a tenner and she had been to Chapel Market and bought herself a new top to wear. She had not had any new clothes for a long time. All her money went on keeping food on the table and putting decent clothes on Dennis' back. She felt good in her new outfit. The top flattered her figure and clung in all the right places. She didn't have a bad figure. She could not afford enough food to get fat she told herself cheerfully as she took another swig of her drink. Being poor had some advantages.

Martin Crayford had been propping up the bar and had offered to buy her another vodka and tonic. She had been pleased at the attention and the money she would be saving and readily agreed. They had chatted animatedly much to the amusement of her pals. They gave her encouraging thumbs up over his shoulder as Adele flirted like mad. She had fallen for Martin very quickly. He took her on to Zanadu's nightclub when the pubs shut and took her home to his neat and tidy flat above a shop in Upper Street after the night club closed. She was surprised at how clean and tidy everything was. She had always imagined bachelor pads to be complete tips. When she had commented on it, Martin had shrugged his shoulders and said that he liked order. Adele thought it would be just a one night stand. She was delighted when he took her phone number and called her up the following day. The sex had been fine, but she could not imagine that it had exactly blown his mind. She did not have much confidence when it came to high jinks in the bedroom. She was amazed that he actually wanted to come back for more. He splashed lots of cash on her over the coming months, bought her expensive presents and had become brilliant in bed. She had relished the attention. He had not turned a hair when she told him about Dennis on their second date. He had been really good with him, too. He was kind and affectionate, and she had never had that sort of relationship with a man before. Jimmy had been a selfish demanding bastard. Martin had got Dennis to help him clean and tidy the flat. He had made it into a game and Dennis had enjoyed dusting and sweeping the kitchen floor. Adele had never thought of doing that. She was really impressed.

Dennis had been such a good boy at first. He was just being awkward now. She had put it down to jealousy on Dennis' part. She thought Dennis did not like sharing his mum's affection. He had been asking about his real dad a lot lately. Adele did not even know where he was any more. He had scarpered when the social had asked him to pay child support.

Adele had said yes straight away when Martin proposed. It was such a relief to have an extra wage to help out. She told herself she loved Martin. She was sure she did. She certainly fancied him like mad. He had been kind to her and Dennis but she had noticed that he had a slightly dangerous edge. She found that very attractive at first. Everyone loves a bad boy she had told herself, it made things exciting. There was nothing she could put her finger on, but he had hinted that he had got into a bit of mischief in his murky past. She found that fascinating. He had also been a bit short tempered. He hated mess and often told her or Dennis off if the flat was untidy when he came home from work. His neat freak streak was becoming a bit tedious. She would not admit that she loved his wallet more than the man himself. He had certainly been generous. She longed for a bit of security and here it was, gift wrapped. He was still generous, good looking and he treated her and Dennis well, most of the time. She reasoned that no one was perfect. So what if he got a bit stroppy from time to time? For the first time in years, she did not have to worry whenever a brown envelope dropped on to the mat. The bills were being paid and there was food on the table, and smart new clothes for Dennis and her. She could even manage a trip to the hairdressers, and had a new young and trendy hair do. That was more than enough.

Adele's mum did not stay around too long, once Martin appeared on the scene. Her mum did not like Martin; she had made that very clear long before the wedding day. If Martin came round to see her at the flat her mum would soon create an atmosphere that was so thick Adele could have sliced it up and tinned it. Just when Adele had got used to having her around again, she had said she needed to get back to Norfolk. It had been so lonely trying to cope as a single mother again once her mum had cleared off. She began clinging to Martin like a life raft after her mum had packed her bags and scarpered. She had been at her wits end. She loved her little boy with all her heart, but   sometimes she had felt the walls closing in and the burden of care was too much to deal with. She had felt old before she had ever even had much of a life. She was still only twenty-four. When Martin asked her to marry him, it had seemed like a fairy tale, the answer to all her prayers. It had all happened very quickly, but it had been very romantic. Her mum had not come to the wedding. They had a very small gathering and a reception at home.

Martin came into the living room. He had been having a shower after work. He worked as an electrician in the Business design centre and did an early shift. He was always happy to look after Dennis, Adele thought fondly. Even though he must have been tired after his early starts every day. He was very considerate. She was lucky to have him. "Heh Dennis, what's all this noise then?" he said softly to the little boy who was still howling loudly.

"I'm sorry love." Adele said apologetically. "I don't know what's got into him these days. He doesn't want me to go to work again. He never used to be so clingy." Martin smiled at his new wife. "Don't worry, babe. It's alright, I'll see to him. We knew it wouldn't be all plain sailing, didn't we? Go on, you get off to work. We'll be fine" Adele smiled with relief. She kissed Martin then turned to her son whose whole body was now heaving with great gulping sobs. She hated leaving him in such a state. "Come on Dennis love, Mummy has to go now. See you soon. Try to be a good boy."

The door slammed behind Adele. Martin knelt down beside his new stepson. "Come on Dennis" he said softly. Dennis stopped crying but his eyes were wide with fear. He looked up silently, with his bottom lip quivering. Martin smiled. It was a nasty, shark smile. "I can see we understand each other," He whispered menacingly, inches away from the terrified child's face. His tone changed abruptly now he knew Adele was out of earshot. "Now, let's not have any of your nonsense. I'd hate to have to discipline you again before Mummy comes back. You know what I'll do to you if you don't do as I tell you."

"Daddy!" Amy Oakland ran and threw herself into Jay's arms. He knelt down, hugged his precious little girl to him, and kissed her cheek. It was good to be home. It had been a tough day. He could not get poor little Dennis out of his mind. He drank in the sweet warmth of his daughter and felt his stress begin to slowly melt away. As he stood up, his little boy Bobby Jay came toddling towards him, a big gurgling grin on his upturned face. Amy went back to her colouring book. Jay scooped Bobby Jay up in his arms and called out to Suzy, who was busy in the kitchen. "Hello Suze, how's your day been? Ooh, something smells good. I'm starving!" He walked into the kitchen with Bobby Jay still in his arms. Suzy looked round, smiled, and kissed both her boys. "Hello hun. It's only a meat pie. One of Kwik Save's finest." Suzy said cheerfully. "Good old mum, she's been supplementing our larder as usual. She said she couldn't fit it in her freezer, so we might as well have it. Bless her; she thinks we'd all starve without her food parcels. It'll be ready in five minutes. You're late tonight."

"Staff meeting" Jay said, struggling to take knives and forks out of the cutlery drawer. It was not easy with one hand. He put Bobby Jay down and he toddled off to find his sister. "I thought it would never bloody end. I'm amazed the whole staff room didn't comment on my rumbling tum." He went to lay their tiny little dining table in the living room. Suzy always insisted that the family ate together round a table. She would have none of this food on laps in front of the telly nonsense. Jay could not help smiling as he watched his wife. Suzy was busy mashing potatoes and dishing up carrots and green beans to go with their pie. He pinched a carrot off a plate and popped it in his mouth. "Oi,!" said Suzy, grinning at Jay and laughing. Jay winked at her, and pinched another carrot. It was good to see his beautiful Suzy looking so happy. When they had met , there had been an instant attraction. Suzy had brought her daughter Ellie May to meet him, as he was to be her class teacher. Jay really wanted to get to know Suzy better, but it was not allowed if he wanted to keep his job. He felt sure that the attraction was mutual though. Ellie May had been a delightful little girl, always happy and bubbly. She brightened up the room as soon as she entered it, just like her beautiful mother. Ellie May loved to sing. Her favourite song had been "You are my sunshine" she sang it so much that she had earned the nickname "Sunny" at school. Jay had been absolutely devastated when Sunny Ellie May had been killed so tragically. He could not imagine the hell that Suzy was going through. He had longed to comfort her, but of course, it had not been appropriate at the time. It was not his grief and professionally he was not allowed to intrude. He had waited for almost a year before contacting Suzy and asking her to go for a drink with him. They had been together ever since. Jay had never been in love before he met Suzy. He had found it difficult to let anyone in. It was different when he met Suzy. Somehow, the sadness inside both of them had drawn them together. They understood one another and an unbreakable bond had been forged. Suzy had been easy to love.

Jay had seen Suzy's pain as a tangible thing in their early days together. Her smiles never quite reached her eyes. Suzy had tried hard to get on with her life, but the devastation she felt at the loss of her child was a dark cloak that engulfed her and sometimes over whelmed her. Grief could be such a cruel master. It never left of course. Jay knew only too well. It could not be tamed, and it would lie in wait like a hungry lion always ready to show its claws and inflict its pain unexpectedly. Birthdays and anniversaries were still hard to get through. Suzy still had bad days. Then Jay could do nothing but hold her, stroke her hair and let her cry. Jay understood the guilt Suzy felt too. He had always felt guilty because he was alive and had not been with his parents when they had been killed. All the "if only's" in the world could not change things. Suzy had confided that she had planned an abortion when she discovered she was expecting Ellie May. If only her bastard of a boyfriend, Ellie May's father Billy, had not stolen the money. Suzy could not forgive herself for that, or for not preventing Ellie from slipping out of her grasp and running into the road that fateful day, straight into the path of a speeding car.

Jay in turn had confided his feelings to Suzy. They had lain in each other's arms and Jay had told her about how lost he had felt, how terrified he had been, lying in a strange bed after his parent's death. He had, in time told her about some of the beatings he had suffered from one set of foster parents. How they had beaten him with a wet towel, so as not to leave any tell-tale marks. Suzy had cried when he told her. It had been her tears that had made Jay realise how lucky he was to have found her.

Things had become much better when Amy and Bobby Jay came along. He saw the smiles light up the whole of Suzy's face, and her eyes sparkled with love. Jay had never been happier. He had grown to love

Suzy's family too. He had always admired the closeness Suzy shared with her family. Her mum and dad, Joycie and Bob and Suzy's brother Robert had welcomed him into the family and he had relished in being part of it all. He finally had the family he had always wanted.
 Suzy's friend Sarah had also been fantastic. He had become good friends with her and her husband Jon. Jay was so grateful to have found happiness and was always careful not to take things for granted. He knew how quickly things could be snatched away.
He tucked into his mashed potato as Suzy put his steaming plate in front of him and tried to push the sad little face of Dennis Crayford temporarily to the back of his mind.

Nina Taylor heard the shower running and considered going in to her tiny bathroom to join the delectable Nico. However, she was too warm and snuggly under the covers to move, and besides, she knew Nico had a business meeting he had to go to. She pulled the duvet up to her chin and smiled. She had never been happier. Nico had told her somewhat reluctantly he did not want to be late. He had been lying next to her at the time, running his fingers deliciously up and down her spine and Nina had smiled, delved deeply into her will power and practically had to kick him out of bed. They had just returned from two wonderful weeks away in Antigua. Nico really spoiled her. He had taken her to Paris for a surprise shortly after they had first started seeing each other. She smiled as she remembered strolling hand in hand along the Champs Elise and admiring the view from the Eiffel Tower. They had done all the touristy things, and then gone back to their hotel suite that had been the height of luxury, and made love in the huge four poster bed. She had felt like royalty. It was the first of many trips away. Nico had to travel extensively for business and he took Nina along whenever he could.
 It had been fabulous to travel first class of course, but Nina was so in love that she would have been just as happy if they had been on a wet weekend in Skegness. She had met Nico Montelli through work. It sounded corny but their eyes really had met across the hotel lobby and for Nina at least, it had been love at first sight. Nico was a very wealthy businessman who often used the Imperial Hotel's conference facilities. He had taken over his family business fifteen years ago and expanded it

beyond his father's wildest dreams. His father Gino, had started a small electronics company in Italy. Now they made computer software as well as electronic gadgetry and sold all over the world. Montelli Electronics were well known for quality products and had an excellent reputation worldwide now.

Nina had been promoted last year to senior receptionist at The Imperial. She was also in charge of bookings and it had been her job to take care of Mr Nico Montelli when he needed the conference suite at the Hotel. Her new position had meant a considerable pay increase, and she was at last able to afford her own little flat. It was tiny, and in the East End of London, where property prices were a lot more affordable. Her miniscule flat was near the Docks and she loved it. It had been a long time since she had a place of her own. She had taken great care of Mr Montelli. He had smiled into her eyes on that first day and she had wanted to whisk him off and give him her undivided attention right from the word go. However, she had tried to remain professional even though it had not been easy. His chocolate brown eyes and lazy smile had been very distracting.

When Mr Montelli had eventually invited her for dinner, she had been powerless to refuse. He had kept inviting her for dinner after their first meal together and she was now on first name terms with most of the Maître De's in London's top restaurants. He had been easy to fall in love with. He was generous, intelligent and always attentive. He had a deliciously mischievous sense of humour and was amazing in bed. Nina had phoned Suzy after their first date and waffled on ecstatically. She had not stopped singing the praises of the wonderful man in her life since they met. She often had long phone conversations with her friend, giving her a blow by blow account of all the glamorous places she had been to with Nico.

Most of the businessmen and executives who used the hotel looked down their noses at the Hotel staff and treated them as if they were beneath contempt. Nico had never been like that. He was always impeccably polite and treated Nina, from day one with kindness. He was never condescending or snobbish to any of the Hotel staff. In fact, he would bellow at any of his colleagues who were rude to the staff. Nina was most definitely smitten. She had been surprised and delighted when Nico actually asked her to have dinner with him on their first magical night together. She had not been sure if she should accept, even though she desperately wanted to. It was considered unprofessional and if the hotel ever found out she were seeing one of the clients her job would be at risk. Mr Montelli was very persuasive however and in truth, she had not needed much persuading. Nina had decided to live dangerously. They had been very discreet and no one knew at the hotel about their relationship. It had added an extra touch of excitement if she was honest with herself.

 She now entertained him in her flat whenever she could. Sometimes he would call her when he was in town and not busy and whisk her off in his chauffer driven car. He had lavished her with presents, and they dined out in restaurants that Nina could never have dreamt of eating in. Nico had told her his company owned a factory quite close to her flat and he would pop in to see her if he could get away from work. They had a wonderful relationship. They laughed together, chatted about everything and when they made love.. Nina shivered at the memories. Nico was tall and incredibly handsome. She thought he was way out of her league. It puzzled her and she could not see what he saw in her. She had not had much self-confidence since her affair with Billy Jameson, and did not realise what a beautiful woman she was. Nico could have had any woman he wanted and yet he had chosen her, she thought incredulously.

Nina snuggled even further under the covers. She could not believe her luck.

It was funny how things turned out, she told herself. There was a time a few years ago when she feared she would end up a lonely embittered woman. After her experience with Billy the bastard Jameson, she thought she would never trust another man as long as she lived. She had met Billy at a rock festival. They had a fantastic weekend together. Nina had been philosophical when they parted, and never thought she would see Billy again. He had turned up on the Isle of Wight where she lived back then, almost a year later. Totally out of the blue. She had been surprised but delighted. She did not know of course that he was on the run from the police. Billy had a gambling habit that had led him to steal from his girlfriend Suzy Pond. Even worse, he had burgled his friend Jonny's house in Islington. When Jonny's father, Victor Mason had come home unexpectedly and caught Billy in the act, Billy had stabbed Victor and left him for dead. Nina was totally oblivious to all of this and had happily set up home with Billy. At first, she had been blissfully happy. They had always had an amazing sex life. For a few months, everything had been just as it was at the festival. They had a satisfying sex life; they laughed together and had tremendous fun. After a while, Billy started asking Nina to do all sorts of kinky things in the bedroom. She had always considered herself broad minded, and willing to try new things. Especially in the bedroom, so she had readily agreed at first. She soon regretted being so compliant. The things Billy had persuaded her to do had been painful as well as undignified. She had felt used, but had put up with it because she really did love Billy. What a complete mug she thought bitterly. She discovered that Billy had secretly been filming her as they had sex. He had turned her into a porn star, selling the films to a vile little man who had peddled her naked antics all over the Isle of Wight. She had become a laughing stock, and the talk of the town.

Still, it was indeed funny how things turned out. If it had not been for Billy, she would never have met Suzy. His ex-girlfriend Suzy Pond had become one of her best friends, along with Sarah, Suzy's friend. Sarah was now married to the love of her life, Jonny Mason.

The three young women had forged an unbreakable bond. They had met when Nina discovered the truth about Billy. She had discovered a holdall Billy had hidden. It had the wallet that Billy had stolen from Victor inside. Victor had a business card in his wallet. Nina had contacted Victor and Jonny, and Billy had been arrested. At the trial, Nina had been appalled when the whole truth had become known. Victor Mason was very lucky to have survived such a vicious attack. Despite everything though, Nina had still been heartbroken when Billy took his own life whilst in prison. He had been sentenced to ten years for attempted murder. He could not cope inside. Although Nina had wanted his balls for tree decorations, she had not wanted him to have such a sad end.

Nina had left the Isle of Wight after the trial. Once again, the local press had turned her into an unwitting celebrity. Every one called her Naughty Nina and she became tired of the sniggering and name calling everywhere she went. She managed to get herself a job in a top Hotel in London, the Imperial. For a while, she had moved into Suzy's flat.

They had had a fantastic time together. Nina had adored Suzy's dear little daughter, Ellie May. Billy had been Ellie May's father. Billy had never accepted Ellie May as his daughter though. Suzy had always refused to tell Billy about her pregnancy. He had made it perfectly clear to Suzy that he did not want to ever become a father and Suzy did not want anything from him. When Suzy had met Billy's poor devastated mother at the trial however, she had softened and had told Violet Jameson that she had a granddaughter.

 Billy's mother Violet had told him he had a daughter whilst he was in prison. Billy had been revolted. Just because Ellie May had Down Syndrome. For Violet, it had been the last straw. She was so ashamed of her eldest son. She had disowned him there and then. She had so wanted him to accept Ellie May. She hoped that little girl would give him something to hang on to, something to live for. Nina felt so sorry for Violet. She had lost both her son and the gorgeous Ellie after the tragic accident. It was such a shame she had blamed Suzy for everything. In her grief and anguish, she had lashed out at Suzy. Now Violet had lost Suzy, too.

 Nina was so happy that Suzy had found happiness again. She had felt so helpless after little Ellie's death. Suzy had been very brave but anyone could tell she was a shadow of her old bubbly self. Until Jay had come along. It warmed Nina's heart to see Suzy and Jay together. They were potty about each other, and now they had two beautiful children together. The kids must be getting so excited about Christmas. Little Bobby Jay was just at the age where he would be aware of what was going on, and Nina had spoken to Amy on the phone just yesterday. She was so excited she could hardly contain herself. Nina knew Suzy and Jay always made it a magical time for them.

Sarah and Jonny had a lovely little girl now too. The little girls were friends, and about the same age. Sarah joked that they were mini versions of Suzy and herself. They certainly looked the part. Suzy's daughter Amy had Suzy's dark hair and the same mischievous smile. While Sarah's daughter Lydia had the same beautiful long red hair that had always been her mother's crowning glory.

Nina turned over in bed. She would get up soon and have some breakfast. She had one more precious day off, and she intended spending it by going to visit Suzy and Sarah. She had presents to take over for the children. She could not wait.

Nico emerged from the bathroom, smelling delicious and looking astounding in a charcoal grey business suit. He had most of his suits hand made in Milan, but this one had been made for him in Saville Row. The suit fitted him beautifully and today he was wearing the silk tie that Nina had bought for him. They had chosen it together on their trip to Paris. Nina had insisted on paying for it, she had wanted to give him something special. He spoiled her so much she liked to reciprocate when she could. He grinned at the dishevelled Nina and leant over to kiss her. "See you later, gorgeous." He whispered. Nina shivered with excitement. His rich deep voice made her tingle. She had been loath to admit it to herself but the depth of her feelings scared her. She knew they made her vulnerable, and it terrified her. After the hurt she had felt with Billy, she was wary.
She heard the front door slam as Nico left. He would hail a cab to take him across London to his office in the West End. No strap hanging for him on the tube she thought, smiling to herself. His chauffer must have the day off, she mused.She sometimes wondered if everything was just too good to be true. She tried to cast aside her misgivings and just enjoy the heady rush of being in love. She hoped that this Christmas was going to be wonderful.

Adam Sandford was disappointed that Sarah and Suzy were not in their little shop today. It was a Thursday and most of the shops in the market were usually closed. There were no stallholders trading on Thursdays so the street was usually deserted. Today however, he had been pleased to see the shutters up as he did his usual tour of Chapel Street. Many traders were open today, as it was the run up to Christmas. He looked forward to the banter he had with Sarah and Suzy far more than he cared to admit. The cheerful women were a real tonic after having to deal with the likes of Cranky Craig Allsop who ran a fruit and veg stall. Old Cranky was still miffed because he had wanted to open a greengrocers shop in Sarah and Suzy's shop unit. He had complained very forcefully about "favouritism" and accused Adam of only giving the shop to "Those young things" because Adam fancied them. Adam had to calm Craig down almost on a daily basis. He always had a bee in his bonnet about someone. He was relieved that he was nowhere to be seen this morning much to Adams relief. He had stopped by as usual for his elevenses only to be met with strange faces however. He tried to hide his disappointment as he walked into the little shop. Marlayna had greeted him with a big smile though, and said that she was Sarah's mother in law. "Well sort of" she added, still smiling widely. Adam warmed to Marlayna instantly. Victor Mason popped his head out from the tiny kitchen area and added, "Hello there, you must be Adam. I'm Sarah's father in law, Victor. Call me Vic most people do these days. Sarah told me all about you, and the kettles on. Sarah and Suzy are playing truant today, and have left us in charge. We are under strict instructions to look after you and ply you with hot drinks. Tea or coffee?"

"Tea please, and don't forget the sticky buns!" said a familiar voice before Adam could reply to Victor. Adam spun round and was delighted to see Sarah and Suzy standing in the shop doorway. They had a lovely looking woman with them who lit up the shop with her beautiful smile. She had a golden suntan, which suggested she had recently been somewhere much more exotic than Islington.

"Hi, what are you doing here? Couldn't stay away, huh?" Adam said when he found his voice. He tried hard to sound casual, but he could not hide his delight.

"Checking up on us?" Marlayna added, grinning from behind the counter.

"No, we just wanted to show off the shop to Nina, and grab a cuppa before we hit the shops. We'll be off to the West End soon. We have to make the most of a kid free day and late night shopping in Oxford Street . Still got a few things to buy for them. We thought we'd make a day of it. " said Sarah. Carrie was looking after Lydia while Sarah did her last minute Christmas shopping. Bob and Joycie, Suzy's parents were looking after Amy and Bobby Jay. Jonny was busy working in the antique shop. Suzy's husband Jay was busy at work. Bonny Ridge had broken up for the Christmas holidays but Jay had gone in to prepare for the new term. Well, that was what he had told Suzy, as he did not want to worry her. Actually, there was a meeting to attend about Dennis Crayford. On the last day of term before the Christmas holidays, Jay had overheard

Martin Crayford shouting at Dennis. He had obviously thought he was out of earshot to anyone else. Adele Crayford had been busy looking at the children's artwork displayed in the school Hall. Dennis had been crying. Jay saw the despicable Mr Crayford grab Dennis roughly and shake him. He put his face very close to poor Dennis, then he heard him hiss, "Don't even think about whinging you little prick, or you know what I'll do!" Jay had just been about to go and intervene when he felt a hand on his shoulder. It was the new head. She had heard too. "No", she said to Jay, "don't rush in, for Dennis' sake. Let's go through the proper channels and nail the bastard's gonads to the wall" Jay's face was red with fury, but he realised that she was right. He was beginning to like Sheila after all. He found it comical that she had used a profanity. It was like watching the Queen deliver her Christmas speech wearing a baseball cap. He had not said anything to Martin Crayford, but they had exchanged looks, and Jay knew that Crayford realised exactly how Jay felt about him.

Martin Crayford had seen the look of hatred in Jay Oakland's eyes, but had not seen any sign of recognition. That was good. That suited his purposes. He had been keeping an eye on Jay Oakland ever since he heard the name. Mr Oakland, or "Mr Oaky" as Dennis called him, was all the kid ever talked about. The way Dennis went on, anyone would think Oaky could walk on water. He had his eye on Jay Oakland all right. He had taken note of his beautiful sexy little wife, too. She had been at the school's Christmas fair, helping on the Bring and Buy table. He had spoken to her and got quite a lot of information. She had been easy to talk to, very amenable. You never knew when information would come in useful. He just had a gut feeling that the do gooding Jay Oakland was out to cause trouble.

Jay had told Suzy he hoped to be home by three from his meeting. He hoped he would not be too long. He wanted to make sure that little boy was safe for Christmas. He was looking forward to unwinding at home later. He had experience of children being abused before, although it was thankfully quite rare at Bonny Ridge. It always upset him and he found it difficult to unwind. He had not been sleeping well lately, lying awake into the early hours worrying about Dennis. Still, he was looking forward to this evening. He was going to order them all a takeaway. He said the girls deserved it after all that shopping. He was not looking forward to the meeting; he knew he would get angry if they did not listen to his opinion. It was time for action and he was not going to be fobbed off about his concerns any longer. He hoped it would not be as frustrating as he feared. Now that Maggie Sharp, the school welfare officer had seen how vile Martin Crayford could be, and the head, Sheila had also witnessed his abusive tone he hoped things would move rapidly. Maggie Sharp had pulled unseen into the school car park one morning last week and had witnessed the odious Martin Crayford shaking Dennis and shouting at him for taking too long to walk along. Poor Dennis had looked terrified and had wet his trousers in fear. When Maggie had approached the sobbing Dennis, Crayford had been as nice as pie and said Dennis was crying because he had an accident. Maggie had not told Crayford she had seen the incident, fearing repercussions for Dennis, but had taken Dennis into her office and given him a spare dry pair of trousers to wear. He had been so upset he had remained in her office all morning. She had of course filed a report and the meeting had at last been called.

Jay was hoping to have the child safely in care before Christmas. It was a shame he would be separated from his mother, especially during the festive period, but she had chosen a spiteful bully for a husband and Jay knew that the child needed protection. He could not explain it at first other than a gut reaction. Now Crayford's bullying behaviour had actually been witnessed he hoped that action would be taken. The longer Dennis was in the clutches of that creep, the more danger he was in. What was wrong with his mother? Why could she not see what was so blatantly obvious? She appeared to be in complete denial, and was steadfastly refusing to have a word said against her husband. Jay had visions of a terrible tragedy taking place if the authorities delayed doing anything for much longer. He knew his hands were tied, procedures had to be adhered to,and that made it all the more intolerable. He could picture the meeting. They would all look concerned, nod a lot, and sympathise. They would waffle on and make excuses for leaving Dennis in his home environment. He had heard it so many times before. They would never remove a child unless they were certain it was in the child's best interests. Even then, in Jay's opinion they waited far too long. It was so frustrating.

Jay could not wait to get home. He knew it was going to be a long and stressful day.

Victor brought out a tray laden down with steaming mugs.

"Sorry, Nina, this is Adam. Be nice to him, he's our market inspector." Sarah added as she picked up a mug gratefully. She winked at Adam. Adam felt his heart turn over but tried not to show it. He looked over at Nina as she handed him a steaming mug of tea. She certainly had a glow about her, and it wasn't just the golden tan. She really was very attractive he thought appreciatively as he sipped his tea. He wondered where she had been to get such a glorious tan at this time of year.

Nina smiled at the man hovering by the shop counter as she passed him his drink. He was tall with twinkling brown eyes. He was grinning at her and he put his tea on the counter and held out his hand to shake. "Hi Adam, pleased to meet you. How do you put up with these two on a daily basis?" she teased as she shook his hand. He had a nice firm handshake. She couldn't help noticing his long sensitive fingers and short clean nails. She liked a man to have nice hands. Nico's hands were always well manicured. She tried to erase the memory of his hands on her back last night and concentrate on her current conversation. Adam was speaking.

"Oh, it's a dirty job, but someone has to do it" he said solemnly. Nina smiled. He seemed like a nice bloke. He had big sad brown eyes, like a puppy dog. He was actually very attractive. Not as blatantly handsome as Nico, but definitely worth a second glance. He obviously had a mischievous sense of humour too, and that was always irresistible.

"Where have you been to get a tan like that in December? You don't get a golden glow like that from South End, or out of a bottle, I know!" Adam added with a grin.

Nina laughed. "Would you believe me if I said I'd been on a sun bed?"

"No" he shook his head and his eyes twinkled.

Nina smiled. "Okay then. I'll try not to sound too smug, but I've just got back from Antigua"

Adam whistled admiringly.

"She's a jammy old cow" Suzy interrupted, winking at Nina. "Drink up; we've got buns that need eating and some serious shopping to get through"

With the introductions over, Nina sipped her tea and admired the shop. She was very impressed. They had done a fantastic job. They chatted for a while and all ate the pile of iced buns that Marlayna magically produced from the little kitchen area. When the last piece of icing had been licked from their lips, Sarah and Suzy said they had better get cracking, and Nina put down her empty mug. The three women strolled off still chatting to get their bus up to Oxford Street.
 Adam watched as they disappeared into the busy throng of shoppers. The market had become crowded whilst they drunk their tea. He could not wait to see them again. Particularly Sarah. He thought her husband Jonny was a very lucky man and he hoped he appreciated what he had.

CHAPTER FOUR

The shops were very crowded in Oxford Street and Sarah, Suzy and Nina
fought their way through the bustle and headed for Debenhams. Sarah
and Suzy wanted to look in on Eleanor Parish, their former shop floor
manager. She had become a very good friend to them over the years.
They could not go to Oxford Street without saying hello. They found her
eventually and she was delighted to see them. "Have you eaten?" she
said when they had finished hugging. "We all had sticky buns this
morning, but that seems like a long time and many shops ago. Must be
the cold weather but I'm starving." Suzy said, smiling. "Oh good, that
settles it. I'm due a lunch break. Please join me as my guests in the
executive dining room." She said, rather grandly. A little smile played
around her lips. Suzy and Sarah exchanged glances. This was a first.
They had never been in there before. "Will they let us commoners in
there?" Sarah teased. Eleanor laughed aloud then and said "Oh, I'm sure
a few of the stuffed shirts will probably have a fit, but who cares. She
winked conspiratorially. " Let's risk it. If anyone kicks off, I'll say we're
having a business meeting."

Nico Montelli finished his coffee and closed the file on his desk. He
buzzed the intercom and his secretary came in. "That was quick!
Monica, can you order me a taxi please. I have had enough for one day.
Why don't you knock off early too. Go home and put your feet up."
"Thank you very much Mr Montelli, but I just popped in to tell you that
your wife and children are waiting for you in reception."

Suzy and Sarah enjoyed being nosy looking around the executive dining
room, as Eleanor knew they would. "How the other half live, eh?" Suzy
whispered to Sarah and Nina. Eleanor smiled. "Actually, the food is
exactly the same as in the main staff dining area. The only real
difference is that we get table clothes and linen napkins instead of
paper and don't have to fight for a table when it gets busy." She
gestured to the three women to make themselves comfortable. They
each had trays with their food on.

Suzy had loved swanning past the Pan Stick People and going into the executive dining area. "Did you see the look on Pan Stick Pam's face?" she said gleefully as they made themselves comfortable around the table. "Yes," said Sarah, grinning over her fruit juice. "I'm surprised she's still here." She lowered her voice a bit and added, "She looks like she hasn't taken her make up off since 1970. I bet she just trowels on another layer every morning. It would need a blowtorch to remove all that slap. She must have a head like a Spanish onion with all those layers." They giggled, even Eleanor. Suzy looked at her in surprise. "Sorry Eleanor, I can't help it, I still feel a bit like I'm back at school around you. It's a bit weird eating with the boss. It still takes me by surprise sometimes that you are so..well, human I s'pose. I still expect you to tell us off and make us get on with our work."

Eleanor nearly choked on her chicken casserole. "I'm not your boss any more remember. You're business women in your own right now. How's it going at the shop by the way? Is business booming?"

The four women chatted away happily over their lunches. Nina told them all about her wonderful holiday and had to explain all over again to Eleanor why she had a suntan in December. Sarah teased her again and said there should be a law against it.

All too soon, it was time to head off again into the crisp cold air and finish their shopping. "Right, sharpen your elbows and let's get to it." Nina said happily, as they stepped outside again after saying their goodbyes. They were heading towards Hamleys Toy shop in Regent Street to buy a few last minute treats for the children.

Nico tried not to look disappointed when he saw his wife Isabella in the reception area. He rearranged his facial features in the lift on the way down from his office. He did not want his children to pick up on any tension between him and Isabella. He loved them dearly but they could not fill the void in his life he had felt before meeting his beautiful Nina. He had hoped to take a taxi to Bond Street this afternoon. That was why he had decided to leave the office early. He wanted to pop into his favourite jewellers and buy something tasteful and expensive for Nina's Christmas present. He had seen a beautiful white gold bracelet that he knew she would adore. He enjoyed seeing the look of appreciation on her face every time he bought her something new. She did not take anything for granted, and had never asked for anything from him. She was very special. Her undemanding nature made him want to spoil her even more. She was certainly not a gold digger. He could spot one of those a mile away. Yes, he had had many affairs over the years, but Nina was different. She had touched his heart as no woman had ever done before. What was the expression she used? We just clicked. That was it; it was nothing he could clearly define. Nina was a striking and beautiful woman but she was not classically beautiful in the way that Isabella was. She was a rough diamond; she had not had wealth or privilege to smooth the edges. It was that rawness about her, the unspoiled freshness she possessed that he had found so appealing. She had been deeply hurt in the past, he could tell just by looking at her. He had been touched when she had confided in him. Nico had wanted to remove the haunting sadness from her eyes. He had not meant to deceive her, had always intended to tell her he had a wife and children. In the beginning, he had not wanted to lose her. As time went on, he had been worried she would not understand. She hated deceit. She had told him her ex-boyfriend had lied to her, and had hurt her terribly. He had longed to confide in her. It had just never seemed to be the right time. The longer they were together, the harder it had become to tell her the truth. He wanted a divorce. He knew it would cost him dearly, but he was tired of living this sort of half-life, pretending every day. Isabella did not deserve it, his children definitely did not deserve it and he wanted a fresh start. He longed to be with Nina. The realisation had shocked him, if he was honest. He and Nina were both from different worlds, but somehow he knew they belonged together. Before Nina had come along, he had been content to coast along, and had become expert in the pretence of his life. Once the Christmas holidays were over, he vowed he would talk to Isabella. New Year, new beginning he told himself.

Nico Montelli's wife Isabella was most certainly beautiful. She was also a very successful and astute businesswoman. She was tall, almost six foot, with long raven black hair and sumptuous pouty lips. In her younger days, when they had first come to London, she had done some modelling. The Ace Face studio had seen her cheekbones and snapped her up. She had been a huge success the camera loved her. She had done catwalk shows and magazine shoots but had found the lifestyle tedious. Now she preferred to be on the other end of the camera lens. She had built up a thriving photography studio and had made a name for herself working with celebrities all over the world. Her days with Ace face studios had made her some very influential contacts and she had been extremely grateful. She had considered herself blessed, she said so often enough to Nico. He always avoided her eyes when she spoke like that. She did not deserve to be deceived and Nico did feel guilty about his betrayal. They had two beautiful children together. Little Marco was seven and looked just like him. Five year old Claudia was every bit as breathtakingly gorgeous as her mother and he knew that one day she would break a thousand young men's hearts.

 They were happy in their own way, but Nico had never been in love with Isabella. If he was brutally honest, he had only married Isabella because she had been pregnant. They came from a small village in Italy and it was expected that they would marry. Nico's family had already been quite wealthy, as his father had always had an astute eye for business. They had lived in the biggest house in the village, in the most affluent area, set high on a hilltop. Nico did not object to the wedding at the time. He had been infatuated with Isabella's beauty and too naïve to know that it was not real love. She looked stunning on his arm and she had been good for his reputation. He was the envy of every young man for miles around, and he liked the way that felt. She was most definitely a trophy wife. Nico had always had a head for business, just like his father, even though he was not experienced in the ways of the world back then. They had a lavish but hasty wedding before Isabella's pregnancy began to show. Isabella had soon become accustomed to living a lavish lifestyle and settled into married life with ease. She had busied herself creating a dream nursery for the new baby. She took endless photographs to help her design just what she wanted. She had discovered a real flair for taking pictures, even in those early days. Nico had tried not to show his irritation at the constant snapping away of her cameras.

Unfortunately, Isabella had miscarried the child she was carrying four months after the wedding. She had been devastated and had sunk into a deep depression. It had taken many months of expensive therapy to help lift the depression. She had concentrated her attentions on building her career as a photographer.

Nico had tried hard to settle into married life. He did all he could to try to comfort his wife after the miscarriage, and support her with her career. They had come to London for a fresh start. Isabella had tried her hand at modelling and had been very successful. He had encouraged her, and when she had said she wanted to concentrate more on photography, he had made all the right noises. Nico had expanded his family's business in London and tried hard to be a good and loving husband. Isabella had also done everything expected of her. She was a marvellous cook. Even though they could afford to hire caterers, she preferred to cook herself when she was at home and was happy to entertain Nico's business clients. She was intelligent and witty and provided entertaining stories around the dining table. However, they both realised as the years passed that something was missing. They had even discussed separation. By that time, though, Isabella was pregnant again. Their sex life was adequate but hardly exciting. Nico always felt as if he was somehow just going through the motions. Isabella was no longer interested in sex now she had conceived. He felt that he was now surplus to requirements. He had fulfilled his purpose and was no longer required.

This time the pregnancy went smoothly and for the sake of their new born son they stayed together. He felt trapped. When Claudia arrived two years after her brother, he felt the noose tighten ever more firmly around his neck. He only slept with Isabella occasionally and she had told him she was still taking contraceptive pills. It surely could not be coincidence that she accidently became pregnant every time he brought up the subject of separation.

They never spoke of it, but Isabella always knew about Nico's other women. She did not make a fuss so long as he was discreet and did not rub her nose in it. In return, she continued to enjoy living a lavish lifestyle. She took the luxuries for granted and Nico felt resentful about it. He could not understand why she was content to accept being second best. She deserved better.

Isabella had a nanny to look after the children. Nico did not approve. Isabella had wanted children so much, and yet now they were here she was too busy with her own career to spend much time with them. They had an apartment here in London overlooking Hyde Park. It was in an exclusive building with a concierge at the entrance and a gym and swimming pool in the basement. The other tenants were all well-mannered and well heeled. They also owned a beautiful town house in fashionable Bath. They owned a holiday apartment in Antigua if the British weather got too much for them, and of course, they could always use the family house in Italy whenever the children wanted to see their grandparents.

Isabella shopped with her girlfriends when she was not working and visited health spas and beauty parlours whenever she felt like it. She wore designer clothes and handmade shoes. The children went to private school close to their Hyde Park apartment and were receiving the best education money could buy. They were polite and had impeccable manners. Isabella was very proud of them, and loved every minute she spent with them. She had worked damned hard to carve out a career for herself, knowing that one day when her children had grown she would have nothing else to fill her life. She should not have been unhappy. She had everything she wanted.
Apart from the love of the husband she adored.

Nico could not help feeling that Isabella was checking up on him. She said she had wanted to surprise him, and wouldn't it be lovely to go and see the Christmas lights with the children. Nico's office was close to Hyde Park and they could walk along Oxford Street and take the children for a meal after seeing Father Christmas in Hamleys. The excited children over ruled his protests that it would be too crowded. "Come on then" he said, grinning at their little faces, and knowing when he was beaten. "But stay close and hold my hand. I don't want to lose you in the crowds"

It was heaving with excited children and their harassed parents in Hamleys. The queue to see Father Christmas stretched the whole length of the shop and had been roped off to avoid the rest of the shoppers. Store staff tried to keep the impatient children who were waiting in the queue happy by demonstrating various toys from the shop floor. The staff all had Santa hats or elf ears on and did their best to jolly every one along. Some were blowing bubbles from a bubble gun, and others were flying remote controlled planes and birds.

Nina felt a bit sorry for them as she came down on the escalator with Sarah and Suzy right behind her. The children were growing restless and their parents looked worn out. No one seemed to be paying much attention to the hapless staff. She was feeling weary now herself and glad that the battle around the shops was nearly over. They had been in almost every shop along Regent Street before reaching Hamleys. Thankfully, this was to be their last stop. Sarah and Suzy were both clutching Hamley's carrier bags with their last minute stocking fillers inside. "I'm so glad we brought the kids to see Father Christmas early aren't you?" Suzy said to Sarah, inclining her head towards the ever-lengthening queue below them. "Oh, not half!" Sarah agreed, nodding. They always brought the children to Debenhams Grotto at the beginning of December. Eleanor Parish managed to pull a few strings for them and got them to the head of the queue before the rush started. The kids loved the VIP treatment and Eleanor loved spoiling the children. "I think it's time for a sit down and a cuppa before heading home, don't you, Nina?" Sarah said, leaning over towards Nina's shoulder.

Nina was not listening. She had spotted Nico in the queue to see Father Christmas. She had thought her eyes were playing tricks on her at first, she was so much in love with him and he was on her mind so often that she seemed to spot him everywhere, but this time it was unmistakably him. Time seemed to stand still as she saw him smiling towards a beautiful brunette and two small children who were with him. The dark haired woman smiled into his eyes and leaned in to kiss him on the lips. The same lips that had kissed hers only that morning Nina thought. She felt her heart constrict and she closed her eyes to erase the image. When she opened them, however, they were still there.

The beautiful dark haired woman had her arms around Nico. As she slowly pulled away from him, it was clear to see that she was quite obviously pregnant.

It was crowded in Ponti's café but Suzy spotted a vacant table. She sent Sarah and Nina to claim it while she queued up for their hot drinks. Nina had been dragged almost forcibly from the bustling store. She had

become rooted to the spot when the escalator had reached the floor and Sarah and Suzy had thought she had been taken ill. She was as pale as milk despite her suntan. For a few moments, Nina debated whether or not to go and confront Nico. Then she thought of those poor innocent little children and thought better of it. She did not want to create a scene here of all places. She could not go without acknowledging him though. He had spotted her across the crowded shop floor and a look of sheer horror had spread across his handsome features. Bastard! How could she have been so stupid yet again? Had she not learned her lesson with Billy? She had seen the look on his face turn to one of panic when she had strode purposefully towards the line of slowly shuffling people. It gave her a brief moment of satisfaction. "Hello Mr Montelli" she had said to him as casually as she could muster. He swallowed and his eyes pleaded with her. She could see the brunette at his side eyeing her quizzically. In an instant the raven haired woman had spotted Nina's suntan and knew it matched her husbands. Nico had just returned from their home in Antigua, allegedly finalising a new business deal. It was obvious now he had not been alone. "Sorry, I don't mean to intrude on your family time" Nina said pleasantly, holding her hand out towards the woman by Nico's side. "My name is Nina Taylor and I work at the Imperial hotel. I've...worked with Mr Montelli for quite a while now." She did her best to smile. She watched intently as Nico squirmed. "You must be Mrs Montelli?" the bemused woman nodded and let go of Nina's hand.
"I thought you must be. Are these your children? Aren't they beautiful. They look just like you, Mr Montelli." She stared at Nico, and he looked away uncomfortably. Nina was relentless. " Lovely to meet you Mrs Montelli. I had no idea Mr Montelli was even married. He kept very quiet about it. Very quiet indeed.... When is your new baby due?"
 Sarah and Suzy stood behind Nina and squirmed almost as much as Nico. In the end, Suzy could bare it no longer and said they had a train to catch. They hustled Nina towards the exit. She burst into tears as the cold air greeted them on Regent Street. It was dusk now, and the Christmas lights twinkled merrily above the road unappreciated by the three women. They had to virtually frog march Nina towards Oxford Circus.

"I can't bloody believe I've let myself be duped again," Nina said as she licked the froth off her hot chocolate. "I feel such an idiot. All I've done is witter on about how ruddy marvellous he is, and all the time he had a wife and two kids, with another on the way. He actually told me they did not have sex anymore. Fool that I am, I believed him. He was so convincing. Oh God, that poor woman! Did you see the way she looked at me? She had me sussed, didn't she? I bet she thinks I'm a right old trollop. Probably just another in a long line. I hope she gives him hell when they get home! What a complete shit he is! Well, that'll teach me to be smug." She tried to smile bravely, but her face crumpled and Sarah quickly passed her a serviette. "Oh Nina, I am so sorry. Why don't you come and stay with me?" Suzy said, letting her own hot chocolate grow cold. Nina allowed her tears to flow down her cheeks and she sniffed and whispered, "I can't. I have to get back; I'm working the early shift tomorrow."
"Well, you're not going home alone. I'll come back with you. I'll ring Jay, he won't mind."

Jay came out of the meeting and headed across the car park towards his car. It was nearly 4.0' Clock and already dark. He could see his breath in the cold air as he walked briskly across the tarmac. The car park was deserted. It was odd seeing the car park and playground with no people in thought Jay; it was usually a busy thorough fare full of parents coming to collect their children. It had a stillness about it that was eerie. The nearby streetlights were lit now, which helped to see where he was going. There were just a few staff members' cars in the car park. It had been a long meeting. Now that social services had been informed, Jay had hoped things would be happening. He wanted Dennis to be the happy little boy he remembered and out of harm's way. Martin Crayford was under investigation. Procedures had to be followed however, Jay had been told. The red tape made his blood boil. Stupid Adele Crayford! She still would not have a word said about her husband and was denying any wrongdoing. They had no proof that Martin the moron had done anything untoward, it was all just hear say, she had told the social workers. How could she be so bloody naive? Jay was incandescent with rage. This was her child, for heaven's sake. Surely, she must have noticed the changes in his behaviour. Seen his bruises? He knew they could not go in mob handed, it had to be thoroughly investigated, but how much more evidence did they need for goodness sake? It was so frustrating for all concerned. They did not want to take Dennis into care unless they felt he was at serious risk, and his mother was adamant that he was safe. The family home was clean and furnished well and Dennis was fed with no obvious signs of neglect. For the moment, social services would take no further action, but would they assured Jay, be keeping a close eye on the Crayford's. Jay was not happy about it, but he was, for the moment, powerless to intervene. Dennis would be closely monitored but Jay felt it was not enough.

As he fished the keys out of his coat pocket, he saw Martin Crayford striding angrily towards him from the shadows. He must have got wind of today's meeting. He had obviously been lurking in the dark recesses of the car park waiting for him Jay thought grimly. Everyone else was still inside drinking coffee in the warmth of the staff room. Jay had made his excuses. He just wanted to get back home. He had done all he could for the time being. Hopefully Social Services would now do all in their power to safe guard that vulnerable little boy. If they did not, Jay knew he would stop at nothing to help that child.

 Martin Crayford was now only a few feet away. Oh great Jay thought sarcastically, just what I need, a car park confrontation. He had tried to be reasonable sitting around the table in the staff room but in his heart he could not understand why they had not locked him up yet. If ever any one deserved to be behind bars it was the vile specimen in front of him. Jay knew that the social workers who were still in side drinking their coffee had been to the Crayford's home. The Crayford's had been informed that social services were investigating , and possibly considering taking Dennis into care as a last resort. Adele had cried and begged them to allow Dennis to stay home. Now here was Martin Crayford, standing with a murderous look in his eyes, inches away from Jays own face.

"Mr Crayford" Jay said curtly, "what can I do for you?"

Martin Crayford's face was set in fury. Jay wondered briefly if this was a look that Dennis was familiar with. If it was, no wonder the poor kid always looked so nervous. It was full of menace.

 "I'll tell you what you can do for me, you bloody interfering prick!" he spat. "I knew it was you who put the boot in with the social services.

You have been a busy bastard, haven't you? The last thing I need is a load of do gooder's splitting my family up! How would you like it if someone took away your kid? My wife is in bits because of you and your bunch of nosy parkers! Keep your fucking nose out of my business!"

 Jay did not bother replying. He would have loved to tell Martin Crayford what he thought of him but he reminded himself he had to remain professional, if only for little Dennis' sake. He walked over to his car and put the key into the lock. Crayford had not finished however. "Don't you fucking walk away from me!" he shouted.

Jay did not have time to turn around or retaliate. Crayford's fist took him by surprise as it connected with the back of his skull. Crayford had been a keen amateur boxer in his teens. He had not forgotten how to throw a punch.

Jay slumped to the ground and clutched at the car door handle in order to try to steady himself. It was then that he felt the blows raining down upon him. He covered his head in vain to try to protect himself but it was too late. He felt a heavy boot connect with his head and then there was nothing but blackness.

CHAPTER FIVE

The phone was ringing shrilly as Nina unlocked her front door. "If that's Nico, I'm not speaking to
him," Nina said determinedly to Suzy as she dumped her shopping bags on the sofa.
 "Shall I answer it?" Suzy said gently, putting her own bags down gratefully.
"No it's okay, I've got to face him sooner or later." Nina said, suddenly brave as she headed for the phone. A part of her still hoped against hope that the whole thing had still been a terrible mistake. She took a deep breath and snatched the phone up.
 "Hello?"
It was not Nico. It was Sarah. "Oh Nina, thank God you're back. I've been ringing for ages. Sorry, but can I speak to Suzy? It's urgent. Something terrible has happened to Jay."

Sarah told Suzy that Jonny was on his way to pick her up, with her mum and dad. He would take them to Bart's hospital. The head teacher had found Jay badly assaulted in the school car park. He was still unconscious. Suzy had sagged to the floor when she had heard the news, clutching the phone with both hands. "Don't worry about the kids, I've got them, they're safe." Sarah added before finally hanging up. Despite the doctor warning her about Jay's injuries, Suzy still recoiled in horror and gasped in shock when she saw the unrecognisable person lying in the hospital bed. She could not believe that this swollen battered and bruised person was her beloved Jay. He had just been brought back from emergency surgery to try to repair his injuries. Suzy and her family had waited anxiously in the corridor until they had seen the hospital trolley being wheeled back from theatre. A doctor had gently taken Suzy aside before allowing her to see her husband. A police officer had also been present. Jay had been viciously attacked from behind, the police officer had gently explained. Judging by his injuries, they could tell that once down on the tarmac of the school playground, his assailant had kicked him repeatedly and stamped on his head. Suzy had let out a little scream when she heard this, and her mum had tried her best to comfort her. Jay had a fractured skull, broken fingers, a shattered eye socket and broken ribs. There had also been some internal bleeding.

The journey to the hospital had seemed to take an eternity. Suzy could not quite take in what had happened. Her dad had sat holding her hand and gently tried to fill her in as Jonny drove, grim faced, across London from Nina's flat. It had brought back horrible memories for Jonny of the day he had found his own father lying in a pool of blood after Billy Jameson had attacked him.

"Oh my God!" Suzy gasped, her hands flying to her mouth, when she was eventually allowed in to Jays bedside. "What has that bastard done to you?" she choked back sobs and rushed to his side. He had not regained consciousness yet. The doctors had told her that it might take some time before he awoke. They were giving him medication to keep him sedated to help him heal. Suzy sat helplessly holding his hand. "Oh Jay, it's Suzy, can you hear me? It's alright darling, I'm here."

Nina had sat restlessly waiting for news. At least it had taken her mind off her own problems. She had made herself a cup of tea, but then decided she needed something stronger so had rummaged in the cupboard and found a small bottle of Jack Daniels. She poured herself a tumbler full and jumped as the doorbell rang. She nearly spilled her drink but managed to steady it and left it on the kitchen counter while she ran to open the door. She hoped against hope it would be Suzy, telling her it had all been a hideous mistake and Jay was fine.

It was Nico. Nina stood and looked at him blankly. She was so worried about Jay and Suzy that Nico was the last person she expected to see. She struggled to regain her composure. "I've got nothing to say to you." Nina said simply, once she had found her voice. She tried to close the door. Nico was too quick, however, and managed to put his foot in the way. "Come in then" Nina said resignedly, as she realised Nico was not going to leave without a fight, "but make it quick. I'm busy," Nina snapped. She strode angrily back in to her kitchen and picked up the tumbler. She took a large swallow and turned to face Nico. The neat whiskey burned her throat and she tried not to pull a face. "Can I have one of those please?" Nico said quietly, indicating the tumbler. Without a word, Nina handed Nico the bottle of Jack Daniels and another tumbler. "Drink up, you're not stopping." she said cuttingly. "Please, let me try to explain" he said, raking his fingers through his thick black hair. It was a familiar gesture. Nina tried not to let it distract her. She was desperately trying to resist the urge to tell him what had happened to Jay. She longed to let him soothe her and tell her everything would be all right, he would hire the best doctors in the world and Jay would make a miraculous recovery. Damn him! She had to remain resolute and not weaken. He was a lying cheating bastard. Hang on to that, she told herself as she took another hefty swig from her whiskey. It was no substitute for a pair of strong reassuring arms around her though. She suddenly felt lonelier than she had ever done in her whole life. She wished she had something to mix it with. She did not even like whisky. It had been Nico who drank it. She had bought this very bottle for him. Now she wanted to hit him with it. Instead she watched as he carefully poured himself a large shot and downed it in one go. He put the tumbler carefully down on her worktop. She was angry not just with Nico but at herself. She was so worried about Suzy and Jay yet she still longed for Nico. She stood up as tall and as resolute as she could. She reminded herself of just how devious Nico had been and she felt all her anger bubble up inside her like molten metal. Her fury made her stronger. He was searching her face, willing her to understand. She was not about to cave in. At last, she found her voice.

"Well, come on then, this had better be good. What was I to you, Nico, the latest popsy in a long line? A bit on the side to break up the tedium of a long meeting? Did it slip your mind that you had a wife, kids? Oh, and another on the way? Let's not forget that poor little baby! Did you ever stop to think what you were doing to those poor innocent little children?" Nina's face was red with anger. She was trembling. She took a deep breath to calm herself.

Nico poured another drink from the bottle silently. His own face was ashen. He sipped his Jack Daniels and put the bottle and tumbler down on the worktop again. "Are you finished? Will you let me speak?" His eyes were pleading with her, but Nina refused to be drawn in. She had to remain aloof.

She stood up as tall as she could muster again, as if by standing tall she could avoid the inevitable hurt. She swallowed hard and blinked back tears. With her arms folded protectively around her, she fell silent.

Nico looked at her, still searching her face. She met his pleading eyes then. She could not help herself. Her face betrayed her emotions, but she would not look away.

He sighed and then he said quietly "I am sorry. Sorrier than you will ever know. I can see how much I have hurt you. I never intended to, I have been a complete idiot. I really, genuinely never meant to lie, or to hurt you. I never wanted to hurt anyone, certainly not you or my children. Or Isabella, my wife. At first, yes, I admit, I was attracted to you, but I never thought it would lead to anything too serious. I was wrong. I realised very quickly that you were special. I knew in the beginning if I told you I was married, I would lose you. You were different from the rest. Yes, there have been other women. My wife Isabella...she knows about them...we do not speak about it, but she is not a victim. She has a good lifestyle; she is a wealthy woman, an astute business woman. She does not need me, or my money. Maybe she has lovers of her own, I do not know. I think she does. I do not know if this child she is carrying is mine, although I will always support the baby. She does not love me. She does not rely on my money. Our arrangement suits us both. Or rather, it did, until I met you. I love you Nina, and I intent to get a divorce. I want us to be together, to build a good life together. It will be a wonderful life, I know it! Anyway, I know it is easy for me to say that now, but it is the truth, please believe me. I was going to tell you about Isabella, but it never seemed to be the right time. I was too afraid of losing you.." Nico had finally run out of steam, and ended abruptly. He raked his fingers through his hair again. He took a tentative step towards Nina, but she recoiled in horror. Nico looked shocked at her response.

"Afraid of losing me?" Nina said incredulously, "Well, guess what Nico? Now you have! Just go away! I hope you get knob rot and your poor wife takes you for every last penny you have got!"

"No! please, Nina, I know you are angry and you have every right to be! But please, don't let this be the end! We have something very special together. Something that maybe only comes along once in a life time! I'll do anything, just name it! We can go anywhere...we could have such a wonderful life together.." he took another step towards her, reached out for her but she stopped him with a hard glare. "Don't you dare!" she shouted, her voice thick with emotion. "You can't give me the one thing, the only thing I have ever wanted!" she said, tears streaming down her face now. She let them, she no longer cared. "I never asked for anything from you… I didn't need expensive presents or holidays or meals out in fancy restaurants, Nico. All I ever asked of you was honesty. Pure and simple. I just wanted to be able to trust you! Now I never will. It's over." "You talk about trust? You haven't been completely honest either, have you?" he said staring at her distraught face. He licked his lips and said quietly but distinctly, "I know about your earlier career as a porn star, Nina. I made it my business to find out all I could about you. I know about your sex videos and I forgive you. Can't you find it in your heart to forgive me?"

Nina opened her mouth and gave a short ironic little laugh. "You're bloody unbelievable!" she spat, "You know about me being a porn star? You don't know anything! Not that it's any of your bloody business but even I didn't know about being a porn star! That was another lying, deceitful bastard! I told you I had a nasty boyfriend. He filmed us having sex with a hidden camera then sold the tapes. Now maybe you will realise why honesty and trust are so important to me. How dare you spy on me! When all the time you were the one sneaking around behind your wife's back! Now a lot of things make sense. Nico, tell me, is there even a factory near here? Or did you just want to visit me here in the poor and very unglamorous part of town to avoid being seen by anyone who might know you?" she could tell by his guilty expression that she was right. She shook her head in disbelief.

He tried one last time, taking her hand in his. She could smell his expensive cologne and she still ached for him. She was furious with herself. He had piled one lie upon another and yet she could not help herself. She managed to wrench her hand from his grasp. "I would like you to go now." She whispered. "You see" she added, "There is an old saying where I come from. If they do it with you, they will do it to you. I am never going to allow myself to be in your poor wife's position. How could I be with you, trust you, knowing you left your children, your pregnant wife? I don't want any part in your life! You say you love me and maybe you do… for now. But what happens in a few years' time when the thrill of the chase has worn off? Will I be the poor wife at home not knowing who you are with every time you go away on business? No, I don't think so. You are nothing but a home wrecker and a treacherous one at that! Now, get out of my flat you lying bastard!" As the front door closed behind Nico, Nina picked up her empty tumbler and hurled it after him with all her might. It hit the door and shattered into a million pieces. She looked at the shards of glass that littered her tiny hallway. Then she sank to the floor and finally allowed herself the luxury of hot bitter tears.

Christmas passed in a blur for Suzy. Jay remained unconscious and Suzy spent as much time as she could by his bedside. She felt guilty for leaving the children but then she felt guilty for leaving Jay when she went home. She wished more than ever that she could be in two places at one time. She was exhausted but she was as ever eternally grateful for all the help and support of her family and friends. They had all pitched in and done everything they possibly could. Marlayna was helping Sarah in the shop and Victor took over at the antique shop so Jonny could act as chauffer whenever he was needed. Bob and Joycie rallied round looking after the children. Carrie looked after Lydia and cooked for everyone when they were all too busy to cook for themselves. Suzy thanked everyone tearfully every day, and they just looked at her blankly and told her not to be so daft.
 Amy had made cards for her daddy to look at when he woke up. Suzy had kissed her and told her that her daddy would love them. She tucked the cards carefully in her bag and took them to the hospital with her. She told Jay all about it, even though he was still in a deep sleep.

Martin Crayford had gone home in a panic after assaulting Jay Oakland. He had lost his temper and had not intended to take things that far. Jay Oakland had still not remembered him when he had confronted him in that bloody school car park. Of course, it had been years since they had met. He had had a different name back then, too. He had been Martin Renwick. Jay had only been what, eight? Martin just a year or so older. Martin had been tall for his age though, and had towered over the little squirt. His mum and dad had been foster parents in those days. No, Jay Oakland had not recognised him, but Martin remembered him all right. He had not changed all that much. He looked different, of course, but he was still a bloody goody goody. He hated the snivelling little bastard as soon as he arrived all those years ago. He remembered his mum telling Martin to be kind to the new boy. He had lost both his parents in a car crash, she had said. Martin had not cared. He hated all these other kids coming to the house. He did not want to share his toys or his parents. He was mad with jealousy. He was an only child before and he liked it that way. He had punched Jay in the stomach that first night. The little bugger had not stopped blubbing once he had gone up to bed. He was afraid of the dark, and had cried for his own mum and dad. He had not stayed with them for long. He would not settle and Martin was glad to see the back of him. As things turned out, he had been the last kid his parents ever fostered. His dad had died of a heart attack two weeks after Jay went back into care. Martin knew it was from all the stress from those ruddy foster kids. He had never been ill before. Jay bloody Oakland had been the most stressful. Martin had always been full of resentment over it. He held all those foster kids and Jay Oakland in particular, directly responsible for his own father's early demise.

His Mum had never been the same after that. Martin had tried his best to comfort her, and be the man of the house, but it was not enough. Then, three years after his dad had died, she had met Harry rotten Crayford and changed Martin's name when they got married. All traces of his dad had been erased, or so it seemed to Martin. He had hated Harry. He wanted his mum all to himself. Harry had tried his best to be a good father to Martin, but it had all been in vain. Martin was never civil to his stepfather. In the end, he had succeeded in driving a wedge between his mother and her new fancy man. They had divorced. Martin had taken it for granted that his mother would immediately turn her full attentions back to her son. However, their relationship was never quite the same, and as time passed, Martin became more and more disturbed. That was what the useless doctors had said anyway. There had been all those visits to the doctor. Then referrals to see a shrink. He did not need their pills and potions. There was nothing wrong with him. His mother had turned into a right old nag. He had been grateful to meet Adele and have an excuse not to see her so often. When he had left home and got his own little place, his mum had always been on the phone, wittering and worrying. He was fine, he was managing and everything was under control. He and Adele would be all right.

Martin was shaking as he washed his hands in the kitchen sink. They were grazed and covered in blood. He did not want to remember his stepfather. He had danced on his grave when he died. He had always had a close relationship with his mother until Harry had come along. Now it was just the two of them again. He could do no wrong in his mother's eyes before him. He had spoiled everything. Then seeing Jay Oakland again and discovering he was still a fly in the ointment had brought it all back.

Adele had seen his blood stained coat of course and demanded to know what had happened. Martin looked up from the sink and smiled to reassure her. "It's nothing. I just had a bit too much to drink after work that's all. Got into a fight in the pub. I'm an idiot. I tell you what, let's go away for Christmas. My mum would love to see us. She gets lonely in that big old house of hers now Dad has gone. How do you fancy a nice few weeks in the country? They've got snow in Kent! A white Christmas! Go on love, say yes. Let's pack our bags and get away from it all!"

"But.. the social services said we had to stay in touch, they won't be happy about us going away, will they?" Adele said doubtfully.

She saw Martin's face cloud with anger. He was intimidating when he looked like that. "Fuck those nosy interfering bastards! I've done nothing wrong. It's all the interfering twats at the school who have put the boot in!" he spat nastily. Adele had never seen this side of her husband before. A flicker of fear ran down her spine. "Who's side are you on, anyway?" he added, inching towards Adele. "We're entitled to a nice Christmas." He said, his voice softening. Adele noticed he was still clenching his fists. She spotted the grazing on his knuckles. It must have been quite a scuffle he had got himself into. She just wanted to keep the peace. She knew he had been drinking. Quite heavily, judging by the smell on his breath. She took a step backwards and smiled reassuringly. She was relieved when she saw Martin's facial features relax. He unclenched his fists. "Of course we are entitled to a decent Chrimbo. You're right," she said brightly, trying her best to placate her husband. "Any way, I bet the social workers won't bother us over the holidays. I'll go and pack right now." she added decisively. She didn't tell Martin, but she would let the social worker know where they were going. She did not want them to have any more ammunition against her.

"Mrs Montelli, your husband is here," the bright-eyed young nurse said as she entered the private room on the maternity unit. "Shall I show him in? I expect he is eager to see the baby."
Isabella sat up in her bed. She ignored the shocked expression on the young nurse's face, as she said firmly, "No. I do not wish to see him, please tell him that and make sure that all the staff know. He is not allowed anywhere near my child. Would you fetch my baby, please? I want to see my son."

CHAPTER SIX

Louise enjoyed strolling along Upper Street towards Camden Passage. All the shops had made a real effort with their window displays and she was feeling very festive. She was heading towards the shop where she hoped Jonny would be working. She was nervous, but had rehearsed in her head what she would say to keep it casual. She hoped he would not suspect that she had planned everything down to the last detail. She could see the shop now. Despite it being a bitterly cold day, she felt her palms sweating. Oh my, he was there! She could see him talking to a customer through the plate glass window. She looked at the pretty window display while he was busy. There was a little green wooden sleigh on display, with presents and a few tin soldiers spilling out of a hessian sack. Fake snow covered the floor and sprigs of holly were placed along the edge of the window to frame the scene. It had all been arranged very artistically and the twinkling fairy lights that lit up the window made it all look quite magical. She waited until the customer came out before she entered the shop.

Jonny looked up. Louise could not read the expression on his face. Did he recognise her? She did not think she had changed that much, but it had been a long time.

"Hello Jonny! Long-time no see! How are you?"

Jonny looked surprised. His glorious face looked right at her, and she felt her mouth go dry. "Louise? I hardly recognised you. What are you doing here?" he managed to say, somewhat warily. Louise licked her lips nervously, and took a deep breath before saying the words she had rehearsed over and over in her head. "I am visiting my parents before Christmas, and doing a bit of shopping." She said, smiling as casually as she could muster. Her heart was racing. Oh, he was just as handsome as she remembered. "Actually, I wondered if you could help me. I'm looking for a present for my mother. She announced over dinner a few months ago that she has always wanted a tiny Schuco teddy bear. She loves the antiques Road Show and she was waffling away to Dad about it. I thought it might make a wonderful present for her if I could track one down. She is usually such a difficult person to buy for! These little bears apparently are now very collectible. She hates perfume and chocolates. I mean, what else is there for mothers? She gave a nervous giggle. "Anyway, do you have anything suitable?" Louise had run out of steam. She had rehearsed her little speech for so long inside her head, trying to make it plausible, that she had made herself more and more nervous. Now she was here standing in front of the still drop dead gorgeous Jonny Mason, all her keep it cool intentions had vanished. She realised she sounded like a wittering ninny. Jonny, however, did not seem to have noticed. He had gone to a glass display cabinet that was jam packed with all sorts of colourful tiny treasures. He took out two items.

"You're in luck. I have these." He said placing two little bears on the counter. Louise feigned interest. Jonny was talking and she hung on his every word. He certainly knew his stuff, she thought admiringly. She tried to remain calm. She hoped she was not flushing. She had an annoying tendency to do that when she was over excited.

"This little fellow is the earliest; you can tell he's a Schuco by his metal arms and legs under the fur. He is in very good condition for his age. He has glass eyes. Some of the later little bears have metal eyes. The other one is actually a perfume bottle." Jonny put down the first bear and picked up the other. "He is more unusual, and he is the more expensive of the two. See, his head comes off, and his body would have contained the perfume." Louise leaned in as close as she dared, pretending to be interested in what Jonny was saying. She drank in his aftershave. It smelled expensive. She did not recognise what brand it was but it was wonderful. Subtle, clean fresh and very sexy.

Jonny, totally oblivious, continued his sales pitch. "First World War soldiers often bought these little bears for their sweet hearts you know. Some girls gave them to their soldier boyfriends to take with them into battle as little mascots..."

Louise was, despite herself, impressed with his knowledge. It had been she, not her mother who had seen one of these bears on the antique road show. She thought it would be a good excuse to set foot in Jonny's antique toyshop. As far as she knew, her mother would not know a Schuco bear if it jumped up and bit her on the arse. However, Louise was determined to purchase one, especially now Jonny had handled it. She would keep it for herself. She knew she would get quite a kick out of having something that Jonny had a connection with. He told her he had purchased the bears recently at an auction. He held out the little bear for Louise to have a closer look. She took it from him. Her finger brushed his as he passed the bear. She tried not to show how thrilling his touch was to her. She studied the bear closely so he could not see her face, which had flushed crimson. It was quite sweet really; it had a dear little face. She picked up the other bear and examined it carefully. She was trying to spin out the time. It felt so wonderful to be near Jonny again. She put the bears on the counter and pretended to be deciding which one to buy. Jonny waited patiently. He was used to customers taking their time. Antiques were costly purchases and customers did not appreciate being rushed. He stood quietly behind the counter, trying not to look as uncomfortable as he felt. Louise made him nervous. She had always been bad news.

"I think they are both so cute!" Louise crooned eventually, "I can't decide. She picked up both little bears again, as if trying to make her mind up. She looked at the price tags. They were both hideously expensive, but she did not care. "You know what? I really can't make a decision. I'm going to have to take them both. I can start my mother's collection. I'm sure she will be absolutely thrilled!"

"Wow, are you sure? They're not cheap," said Jonny. "Far be it for me to talk a customer out of a purchase, but I'd hate to be seen as a pushy salesman."

Oh, he was just as wonderful as she remembered, Louise thought wistfully. If only he was free. She could not leave the shop without trying to find out. Maybe by some miracle he had divorced she mused. "It's fine Jon. If you can't go mad and splash a bit of cash at Christmas, when can you? I want both of them. Could you possibly gift wrap them for me please?"

"Of course" Jon set to work, relieved to have something to do. Louise wrote a cheque and took her time in order to spin out her precious minutes in the shop.

"So, how are you?" she said eventually, as she ripped the cheque from its book. Jon smiled. Louise felt her heart flip. "Still happily married, thank you," he said a bit curtly, she thought. Her face fell. She could not help herself. "I am so sorry for all the embarrassment I caused you back in the day," she blurted out quickly. Jon said nothing; he was still finding the boxes to wrap the little bears in. He felt his cheeks colouring, and he took his time looking for the boxes, in order to hide his embarrassment. "It was a long time ago," he eventually said dismissively.

"Oh, I know, and no doubt a lot of water has passed under the bridge since then, blah blah blah..but, you know, even so. I was a nightmare, and I am really really sorry. Mortified." She grinned mischievously, and added, "I even quite like sausage rolls now."

She was referring to a party at Jonny's house long ago, when he and Sarah had just met. Sarah had brought her mums homemade sausage rolls along. Louise had been very snobbish and made spiteful remarks about it. She was delighted now when Jonny laughed. It sent shivers down her spine. He had found the boxes he was looking for and placed them on the counter. She watched Jonny as he wrapped the little parcels in red tissue paper. His fingers were slim and his nails short and clean. Beautiful hands to match his beautiful face and body. She pictured those delicate fingers tracing the contours of her own body. Jonny handed over the wrapped parcels, snapping her back to reality. "I do love a sausage roll still. Sarah's mum makes the best in the world. Anyway, don't worry about what happened back then. It really was a long time ago. Forget it. I have. I hope your mum loves her presents." He had said his wife's name. Louise was surprised how much it hurt. He said her name so tenderly. Like a caress.

"Can I buy you lunch to make amends?" she said hopefully. Jonny looked even more embarrassed. Damn, Louise wondered if she had pushed her luck too far. She had never had much patience.

"Sorry, but I can't leave the shop. Anyway, there's really no need." He did not want to encourage her, but was trying to be polite.

"Another time perhaps?" Louise said, trying to cover up her own embarrassment now. She realised she had made a fool of herself yet again.

"Perhaps" said Jonny, trying to be tactful. He just wanted her to go away now. She was still like an irritating wasp the way she always used to be. He had longed to flick her away even then, and he had an overpowering urge to do just that now.

"Okay, er..well, nice seeing you. Have a merry Christmas"

Louise took her parcels and left. Jonny let out a huge sigh of relief as the door closed behind her.

Jonny could not believe it. He did not think he would ever see Louise double barrelled whatsit again. He had seen more than enough of her to last him a lifetime. She had nearly caused a break up between him and Sarah back when they first met. She had been a stuck up little madam who thought that Sarah was not good enough for him. He had hardly recognised her. He had heard that she married well. He still saw her father sometimes, as he too was an antique dealer. Her father, Gregg Green, was also a business pal of Jon's dad Victor. Gregg had married a society girl called Marrissa Blakely. The Blakely Greens only had one child, Louise. She had always been spoilt rotten. They had sent her to the City of London School for girls. This private school in the Barbican was full of toffee nosed girls with wealthy parents. Hers had certainly given her everything she had ever asked for. Jonny had been introduced to her when he was in his teens and she had been a thorn in his side until he had married Sarah. Louise looked like she had been polished up like a shiny new diamond. She had lost a lot of weight and her clothes were expensive and tasteful. As a teenager, she had carried a lot of puppy fat, and always seemed to wear clothes that were a size too small. She had worn too much make up and looked like a cheap hooker. Now she looked glossy and svelte and her clothes were tasteful and classically cut. She had an elegance about her that had been sadly lacking back in her school days. She had matured well, he thought charitably. She seemed to have lost her spiteful edge, too. Even though she still managed to irritated him slightly. She was just so, what was it? Pushy? She had certainly improved with age however. He smiled to himself. He would not mind banking on the fact that Sarah would not see her in quite such a good light. Sarah believed that leopards never changed their spots. He would not mention it to her. She had enough on her plate right now, what with poor Jay still being unconscious in hospital after his assault. He did not see any reason why he should upset her, especially at the moment. He still adored his wife and would never do anything to hurt her. He hoped that he would not have to see Louise again anyway.

Jonny rearranged the contents of the glass cabinet where the little bears had been and heard the shop bell tinkle again. He locked the cabinet and looked up expectantly. It was Louise. His heart sank. Did she never give up?

"I thought if you can't come out to lunch, I'd bring lunch to you." she said, somewhat sheepishly. "Don't worry," she added quickly, "I won't stay. Just to say, well, no hard feelings, I hope. Sorry I couldn't find any sausage rolls." She put a huge beaker of piping hot soup on the counter and a fresh crusty baguette next to it. They smelled divine. Jonny felt his stomach rumble. He had not eaten since seven that morning, and he had forgotten the packed lunch that Sarah had made for him. It was still sitting patiently in the fridge for him at home. He had been thinking about closing the shop and nipping home to get it. He did not want to miss any customers that were out Christmas shopping though. He had been busy this morning. He had sold quite a few items. Jonny smiled ruefully. Maybe she really had changed. He felt a bit guilty for finding her irritating and thinking she might still be a scheming little minx. "Actually, you're a life saver" he said gratefully. He opened the steaming soup. "I'm starving, and I forgot my lunch today. Please, don't feel you have to rush off." He inclined his head towards the beaker of soup that Louise still held in her hand and added, "It's far too cold today to drink that outside. I've got another stool behind here somewhere."
Louise smiled and gently pulled off the lid on her own soup beaker. Things were going much better than anticipated she thought, happily.

Christmas had passed in a blur for Suzy. She had tried to put on a cheerful face for little Amy.
 Amy had cried and had wanted to see her daddy on Christmas morning. Suzy had blinked back her own tears and gently tried to explain that the doctors had given Daddy some special medicine to make him sleep. Sleep would help make him better, she had told her gently. Amy had nodded bravely and hugged her mother. "I hope that sleepy medicine works very quick. I need Daddy very badly." she whispered into Suzy's hair. "I want my Daddy back. I want him back ever so much mum."

Jay had not yet regained consciousness and Suzy was frantic with worry. The doctors were still giving him drugs to keep him sedated so his body could recover from his injuries. They had however, reduced the medication, hoping that Jay would begin to wake up. So far, he had not. Suzy had spent all afternoon on Christmas day by Jay's bedside. Her dad

75

had come to take her home after visiting hours were over. She longed to hug her children close and watch them playing with their presents but it was hard to wrench herself away from her husband's bedside. "Come on love" Bob Pond told his daughter gently, "You can't do anymore here tonight. Let's get you home."

Suzy reluctantly kissed Jay goodbye. As she pulled on her cosy winter coat, she heard Jay groan. "Jay?" she said, rushing back to his bedside and taking his hand, "Jay, it's Suzy. Can you hear me?"

Jay's eyes flickered. Bob Pond opened the door and called for a doctor. Jay opened his eyes and blinked to focus. He looked at his wife and smiled then winced as the movement hurt. "Hello sweetheart" he whispered hoarsely to a tearful Suzy.

Sarah put the phone down and beamed at her family. They were down stairs sitting around Victor's fireplace. They had been playing charades. They had all tried to make an effort for Lydia's sake but it had been hard to carry on and have a normal Christmas. They had all been too worried about Jay. They all felt guilty for enjoying themselves while Jay was in hospital and Suzy was so frantic with worry.

Suzy was beside herself and Sarah hated to see her friend so anxious. She had visited the hospital often after work and had been shocked by Jay's appearance. She had seen her mother covered in bruises so many times but Jay's face was swollen and unrecognisable. She had tried to stay strong for Suzy's sake, but seeing Jay with his head shaved and tubes coming out of him had been so upsetting. The person that had done this to him was a monster. Sarah had shivered knowing that he was still free and roaming the streets somewhere. She had told Suzy not to worry about anything other than Jay. She had it covered, she had added sincerely. It had been a lot of effort though. Sarah was worn out. She had not been sleeping, as she went over and over everything in her mind when her weary body hit the pillow. Would Jay make a full recovery? Would the police ever track down the bastard that did it? Had she forgotten any of the orders at the shop? Would she remember to order the ribbon that was nearly out of stock? She just could not seem to switch off. It had also been manic in the shop right up to closing time on Christmas Eve. Sarah had been busy getting orders made up. She was delighted that they were doing so well with their business of

course, but it had been exhausting. Luckily, Marlayna and Jonny were both excellent cooks, and Sarah had been able to put her feet up and enjoy playing with Lydia and being with her family on Christmas day. She had just spoken to Suzy. "Oh it's brilliant news!" she exclaimed excitedly, as she hung up the telephone, "Jay has regained consciousness, and the doctors say he will be fine! Suzy is so excited! It's the best Christmas present ever!"
Carrie was thrilled and got up to hug her daughter. She had kept quiet all day about the pains in her chest she had been getting again.

Adam Sandford opened the tin of Quality Street on his coffee table and took out another chocolate. He unwrapped it and popped it into his mouth. He wondered what Sarah Mason would be doing now. Probably having a wonderful Christmas day with her family, he thought enviously. This was his second Christmas spent alone. His brother had invited him to spend the holidays with him and his wife and kids, but Adam did not want the kids to think of him as the sad uncle with nowhere else to go, so he had declined. He had not wanted to intrude on their family time either. His brother Dan and his wife Lizzy had been really kind since he had split up with Angie, but he was beginning to feel like the sad sack that people only invited out of politeness to any social gathering. It was embarrassing. He might as well have "Reject" tattooed on his forehead. He did not feel sorry for himself it was just uncomfortable when other people obviously felt sorry for him.
He wondered if Angie was having a good time partying with her oafish new boyfriend.
 Adam had met Angie at the gym and they had chatted together while they worked out. He had finally plucked up the courage to invite her for dinner and had been astonished when she had said yes. Very quickly, Adam realised he was totally besotted with Angie. She was clever, witty and articulate, with an amazing body that she had honed to perfection in the gym. They had enjoyed an exciting love life and Adam felt as if he had won the lottery. He could not believe that such an incredible woman would be interested in an ordinary bloke like him. Angie worked in an advertising agency in the West End. She earned a very good salary and he loved her independence and confidence.

77

Adam had trusted her implicitly. After their lavish wedding, they had settled in Islington. Adam had lived in the borough all his life and Angie thought it was a trendy and vibrant place to live. Angie's parents had helped them out with a deposit. They had bought a little flat in Amwell Street. It was on the top floor of a conversion in a wonderful old Georgian house. It was within walking distance of Chapel market where Adam worked, and was easy for Angie to commute to her office in Regent Street. Everything had been blissful for five glorious years.

Until the terrible day when Adam had come home at lunchtime to get some paperwork he had forgotten. He had walked in to find Angie tumbling on their Axminster carpet with her personal trainer. For a split second, Adam had not been able to take it all in. He had stood in the doorframe, rooted to the spot. Angie had looked up, squeaked in shock and quickly stood up, frantically trying to cover herself and mumbling apologies for having been caught in the act. She was completely naked, as was the muscle man who had been Rogering her from behind. He did not even have the decency to cover up. He had actually stood there, with his tackle out, grinning and smirking at Adam's mortified expression. It was that stupid look on his moronic face that had galvanised Adam into action. Adam had sworn loudly and swung an almighty punch at the moron's still grinning mush. It had landed with a satisfying thwack on the moron's nose. Angie screamed and an undignified brawl had ensued, with Adam and the moron rolling around, and all their treasured possessions crashing down around them.

The muscle bound moron had eventually left, dishevelled and bruised. Angie, now wearing a robe, had perched on the edge of their black leather sofa tearfully while Adam got his breath back and wiped his own bloody nose.

It had been the end, of course. As far as Adam was concerned, there was no turning back. Angie had told Adam that he could keep the flat, but he knew he would never be able to erase the image of Angie and the muscley moron from his mind. Every time he came home, he would see the pair of them going at it on the living room carpet. He knew it would eat him alive, so he had packed his bags and for a short while, he had suffered the indignity of moving back in with his old mum. His mum Peggy was an absolute diamond, and had made him very welcome, but she did have a tendency to treat him as if he was five years old. He had spent lonely nights in his old bedroom in Emberton Court. It looked much smaller than he had remembered. It still had his old Arsenal pictures on the wall. It had taken a year to sort out, but the flat in Amwell Street had been sold. He and Angie had split the proceeds and he now had a one bedroom flat in Granville Square. It was still close to work and very convenient for Kings Cross station if he wanted to travel around anywhere. He was trying to move on now. The Granville square flat had been in a right old state when he had bought it. There would have been no way he could have afforded it if it had been in a decent state. Even with the generous deposit from the sale of their marital home. He had spent every spare moment doing work on it. He had called in a few favours from some of his old school pals and had a lot of work done on the cheap. It was handy having mates who were electricians and plasterers. The work had been a great distraction. He had not wanted to admit to himself or anyone else how completely devastated he had been at Angie's betrayal. He had tried drowning his sorrows at first. He had never been that much of a drinker though. All that had achieved had been some almighty hangovers and some embarrassing situations waking up next to strange women. For the past year, he had been almost teetotal and had less social interaction with women than the Pope. It had saved him a lot of heartache but he had to admit it now, he was lonely. The flat looked very smart, but what good was that, when he had no one to share it with?

He changed channels on the television, dipped into the Quality Street again, and settled down on the sofa.

Louise Bingly Warrington forced a smile on to her face as she tried to entertain her house full of guests. It was 8pm on Christmas day and she was tired. There had been the elaborate breakfast early this morning, with smoked salmon and Bucks Fizz. This had been followed by the visit to church whilst the turkey was cooking. Louise had no interest in religion if she was honest, but it was Rupert's family tradition to attend both midnight Mass and the church service on Christmas morning, so she had to go along with it. After the enormous three-course lunch, they had opened presents and now several carloads of revolting relatives had descended. Louise was expected to be the hostess with the mostest and feed and entertain them all. She had had to stand, shivering on the

79

doorstep as cars scrunched along the gravelled driveway, smiling like an idiot and welcome them all in. Her face ached with all the smiling as well as her feet in the new and utterly impractical high-heeled shoes. She could not wait for the whole thing to be over. They were all tedious boorish oafs that Rupert was fond of. Mostly his work associates and all they did all day were talk shop. It was all she could do to stifle her yawns. Their wives and girlfriends were not much better. Some of them were professionals too and Louise had nothing in common with any of them. Tomorrow she was expected to smile her way through a visit to her in laws. She knew they would have only one topic of conversation, was she expecting their grandchild yet? She just wanted to run away and scream.

She longed for her bed. She had put the little teddy bears on her bedside table so they were the first things she saw when she awoke each morning. She wondered wistfully what Jonny was doing right now. She would have traded ten years of her life to be with him.

Nina had to work on Christmas day, and she was very grateful. She had been so busy she had not had a moment to dwell on Nico, or what he might be doing. An enormous bouquet of flowers had been delivered for her at the hotel. There had been no name on the note, but Nico could only have sent them. He always used the same florist. The card simply said "Thinking of you"

"Wow, aren't you lucky! They are gorgeous!" Ginny, the chambermaid had said admiringly when she had seen them.

"Take them home with you" Nina had told her. "I don't want them."

Nina had put her name down on the staff rota to work on New Year's Eve, too. However, the hotel manager had put his foot down and insisted it was not fair to expect Nina to work on Christmas day, Boxing Day and New Year's Eve. Despite her protests that she did not mind, he had told her she was to go out and enjoy herself. "I don't want some union official saying I exploit my staff!" he had added jovially. Nina had no choice but to give in gracefully. She was dreading it though. Christmas day had not been too bad. She had been rushed off her feet most of the day. The staff had all been given a full three course Christmas lunch so she had not had to worry about cooking or eating alone. Boxing Day had been just as hectic. She had had hardly any time to think about lying deceitful Italian men, she thought bitterly. The thought of New Year's Eve at home alone however was enough to turn her to drink. She pictured herself watching some pathetic countdown to midnight show drinking vodka and tonic in her pyjamas. It was not an enticing prospect.

When Suzy had rung to invite her to a party, she had reluctantly accepted. She didn't want to be the sad lonely spinster who tagged along to any social event with her married friends. Suzy had called her a daft old bat when she had protested about being a spare part. "It's the market traders new year knees up. It should be a laugh. Our tickets all say plus one, so you can be mine. Jay is not quite up to the hokey cokey just yet. I was going to stay at the hospital with him, but he won't hear of it. So you'll be doing me a favour really."

Adam Sandford had been pleased to see Nina again. He had been loitering by the buffet table self-consciously when Suzy had arrived with her friend. He had very nearly stayed at home, but the thought of yet another evening wading through the tin of Quality Street was just too depressing. Sarah looked gloriously happy with her husband. They were already on the dance floor, wrapped in each other's arms. Sarah had given him a wave and a smile when she got there. She had introduced her husband Jon. He looked like a decent sort. They had had a quick chat and then gone off to have a dance. Adam had to grudgingly admit they looked very good together out on the dance floor. Suzy was already chatting to one of the market stall traders that she had known since she was a little girl. Her friend Nina was standing by the buffet table. Nina picked at her paper plate full of party snacks and Adam could tell she felt just as lost as he did. He handed Nina a large vodka and tonic. She took it gratefully and had a large gulp. Adam grinned at her. "You look like you really needed that."

"Oh, believe me, I did. It's not easy being single, is it?" she blurted out. "Oh, woops, me and my big mouth. Sorry, didn't mean to put my foot in it. You could be here with some gorgeous special person for all I know." she added, blushing. She put down her paper plate. She wasn't hungry, she had only picked it up to look busy.

"No, don't apologise. You're right. It's not easy. I'm afraid I am here all alone too. I feel like a spare part, truth be told. I don't think I've got any single friends left anymore. I always feel like the sad sack at social occasions. You know, the one with reject stamped on their forehead." Nina couldn't help smiling.

"You sound like you have had one or two bitter experiences." Nina said, laughing. She was feeling a bit tipsy already. This was her third drink in quick succession. "Fancy topping up my glass and playing relationship trumps?" she drained her glass and added, "You can go first if you like. I'm a good listener. I think that maybe we should form a sod em club. What do you say?" Adam laughed. "Same again?"

Adam steered Nina to a table after refreshing their drinks. He was actually beginning to enjoy himself. He could see Sarah on the dance floor still in her husband's arms and he did not even feel a twinge. Well, not much of a twinge. "Come on then" Nina said, sipping her vodka, "Tell me your life story."

"Well, okay, you asked for it. I married a beautiful, sexy goddess who I thought was the woman of my dreams. I couldn't believe my luck actually, and wondered what she saw in me. Anyway, I was blissfully happy for several years. Five, actually. Then I came home unexpectedly and found her rolling around on the carpet with another bloke. Now I know why they call it shag pile." He added ruefully.

Nina winced. "Ouch. Sorry." Adam sipped his pint. "Don't be. I'm not sorry any more. Bitter and twisted, maybe, but not sorry.." they both laughed. "Go on, your turn." Adam said, putting down his pint to give Nina his full attention. Nina smiled sadly and sipped her drink.

"I thought I had met Mr wonderful. He was Italian. Tall, dark, handsome.." Adam groaned. Nina nudged him.

"...and he treated me as if I was the only woman in the world...he was also very wealthy, bought me lavish presents, and took me on luxury holidays. Remember my tan when I first met you? Well, that was courtesy of him. But to be honest I was so besotted I didn't care about that. I couldn't stop singing his praises. Makes me feel pretty stupid now, because he was married with two kids and another on the way. Remember that day when we were first introduced, and I was going shopping with Suzy and Sarah?" Adam nodded.

"Yes, well, I was prattling on about my Mr wonderful all ruddy day. Then who should we spot in Hamleys? Yep, Mr conniving, cheating bastard, in the queue for Santa's grotto with his wife and two innocent little children."

"Oooh, that must have hurt. Think we're about even Stevens on the conniving ex front my friend." Adam said, taking another generous gulp of his pint.

Nina raised her glass. "I hate to do it to you, but I can trump even that." They clinked glasses. Adam was intrigued.

"Go on then, I'm all ears."

"My ex, long before the Italian stallion was called Billy. Or, to be more accurate, Billy the bastard. He was a right charmer. He was the love of my life before the Italian stallion. He actually filmed us..well, you know... doing it, and the treacherous bugger sold the tapes. He turned me into an unwitting porn star. I got my own back though. I tied him to the bed and put cheese wire round his meat and two veg.." Adam nearly choked on his pint. His eyebrows had risen alarmingly, and Nina couldn't help grinning.

"Sorry, have I shocked you?" Nina said, giggling. She was feeling quite merry now.

"Shocked me? No, terrified me, yes.." Nina looked into Adam's twinkling brown eyes. He looked back at her green eyes. They both roared with laughter. A friendship had most definitely been forged.

They chatted together happily for the rest of the evening. They even had a dance together.

At the stroke of midnight, Adam kissed Nina lightly on the lips. "Happy New year. Here's to the sod em club" he whispered.

CHAPTER SEVEN

"Well, you're a sight for sore eyes! We've missed you!" Adam Sandford said. It was early in February and Suzy was back at work. Jay was still in hospital, but improving every day. Suzy beamed at Adam. "Oh, it's lovely to be back! Thanks, Adam. I feel as if I've been gone for a hundred years. I hope you've brought us something calorie laden for our elevenses! I've missed my sticky buns."
Adam held up the box from the bakers and said, "I have indeed. Get that kettle on smartish."
Sarah popped her head out of the little back room. "Kettle's on! Bags I the biggest sticky bun!"
Adam grinned. He had so far played down his new found friendship with Nina. By mutual consent, they pair of them had agreed to keep things that way. Suzy and Sarah did not know that Adam and Nina spoke regularly on the phone and had agreed to go out if either one of them needed company. It had been nice not to feel pressurised Adam had thought. They had a relaxed time together and laughed a lot. It was purely platonic. Adam felt content and Nina was like a breath of fresh air in his sorry excuse for a life. He did not want to admit to himself just how much he looked forward to hearing Nina's voice each time she rang him.

Marlayna put down the telephone and Victor noticed the worried look on her face. "Everything alright?" he said, creases of concern crinkling his handsome features. Marlayna touched his cheek lovingly. "I hope so. That was Cecilia." Cecilia was Marlayna's former next door neighbour. Marlayna had rented out her house in Sekford Street when she had moved in with Victor. Unfortunately, the tenants were proving to be more trouble than they were worth. I think I am going to give Wesley and his charming blue haired girlfriend notice to quit. Poor Cecilia, she cannot take much more. They have been having another all-night party. Cecilia said the police were round and some of the guests were arrested for taking drugs. Maybe I should sell the house and be done with it." Victor shook his head. "Oh that seems a shame. If you sell it, some greedy avaricious developer will get their hands on it, and carve it up into horrible little flats no bigger than rabbit hutches. Then poor Cecilia will have more noise and disruption, and yet more tenants to deal with." He kissed Marlayna. "Ring Cecilia back. Tell her not to worry. Give Wesley three months' notice and we'll work something out."

Louise was trying hard to settle back into a routine now the Christmas festivities were finally over, but she was restless. Rupert had gone back to work in the first week of January, and she found herself ever since wondering from room to room in the big house trying to find something to occupy her time. Even though her parents had insisted she go away to university, she had never been terribly academic. She knew her father in particular had been very disappointed by her lack of drive and ambition. She had just about scraped a third in her degree in Social Sciences. She had been far too busy going out partying to concentrate on her studies. When she had married Rupert, it had seemed very attractive when he had said she did not need to work unless she wanted to. She had pictured herself swanning around town in the sports car he had given her. She had loved the idea of meeting her friends for lunch, and shopping for clothes and trinkets. The reality was just plain boring. Her friends were all either working full time or stuck at home with horrid little ankle biters. One or two had nannies, so could go for lunch if they chose to, but they preferred spending their free time at the gym or spa. She had gone along at first but their main topic of conversation had been their children, or the cost of children's clothes or schooling and she had felt excluded. The wealthy women in the village had invited her to endless coffee mornings, but they had been even more horrendous. Stepford wives, displaying their baking skills and showing off about the fabulous homes they lived in, with their yucky, sticky, screeching children in the background. Louise had politely feigned interest at first but now always chose to ignore the invitations. She was not popular with the village women as a result but did not care. Now Rupert was hinting again about trying for a baby. He was desperate to become a father. Louise had been horrified at the prospect. It was bad enough having to endure her in laws constant hinting for grandchildren, without Rupert badgering her as well.

Her husband was trying to turn her into a stay at home mother, wearing a floral pinny, content to breast feed and make cupcakes all day. Maybe she should start job hunting. Anything had to be better than the good little housewife scenario. She had suggested it to Rupert before Christmas, but he had just frowned and said "What's the point darling, you'll be pregnant soon with a bit of luck." Louise shuddered at the memory. She kept her contraceptive pills very well hidden but never forgot to take them every day. She did not want to risk any accidents. When the telephone call had interrupted her thoughts, it had been a relief. She snatched up the telephone.

It was her father. He sounded strained and asked if Louise could come back to London as soon as possible. Her mother had gone for tests at the hospital a week ago and had just received the results. She had been diagnosed with pancreatic cancer and was asking for her.

Louise was worried about her mother of course; the news was a great shock. It was a relief however to have a valid excuse to leave Rupert for a while. All his baby talk was making her edgy. He had a glint in his eye permanently now, and dragged her off to the bedroom at every available opportunity. She had only been back in Shropshire for a few weeks but the cloying confines of domesticity were already making her long to escape again. The constant pressure from Rupert to conceive was not exactly helping her mood.

She put her Louis Vuitton suitcase in the hall of the home where she had grown up. There were the familiar roses in her mother's favourite vase on the hall table. The smell of roses always reminded her of home. She followed her father into the living room and kissed him on the cheek. "How is she?" she asked gently. Her father looked older, and his face was creased with worry. He had always been devoted to his wife Marissa and he looked like a puppy that had lost his master. He sat down wearily in his favourite armchair and sighed.

"She's sleeping at the moment. She looks a lot better than I do, actually," he said ruefully. Louise patted her father's hand reassuringly. "It will all be okay dad, don't worry. Mummy has a cast iron constitution. I know she will recover. Nothing beats mum." She saw how doubtful her father looked, and added, "I can stay for as long as you need me."

Louise headed for the kitchen to make tea. She was troubled by her father's manner it was so unlike him. He adored his wife, but had always seemed so strong and in control. It was unsettling to see him looking so out of character. He seemed to have crumbled without her mother's influence. In all the years they had been together, which must have been what? nearly Forty, years? They had never spent a night apart. Even when Louise had been born, her father had proudly remained at his darling Marissa's side. Being present at the birth had been most unusual back then.

 Louise felt sorry for her father and her mother, yet she felt happier than she had for a long time, despite her anxiety. She wondered when she would be able to slip out for a few hours. She could not wait to see Jonny Mason again.

Jay Oakland was restless. He longed to go home. He was feeling much stronger, far less battered and bruised. He looked in the mirror now and recognised himself again. For a while, the puffy faced person looking back at him had been a stranger. Now the swelling had gone down and the bruises had faded he was itching for normality. He yearned for his own bed and all the other comforts of home. He was disgusted that Martin Crayford had not yet been arrested. Something kept niggling at him about Crayford, and he could not put his finger on it. He knew Martin looked familiar. He had not realised before, but he had a lot of time in hospital to mull things over. He was still very worried about poor little Dennis. Social services were also deeply concerned. It appeared that the family had done a runner. No one knew where they were. The police had not been able to trace them so far despite making extensive enquiries. His mother swore she did not know where he had gone. Jay knew he would not be able to relax so long as that brutal bastard was loose on the streets. Who was he?

It was always quiet in the antique shop after the Christmas festivities and Jonny was meant to be taking advantage of the lull in trade to catch up with some paper work. However he could not concentrate. He was in a dilemma. Jonny had been surprised when Louise had turned up again. He had put her out of his mind; he had been too wrapped up in all the Christmas activities at home with his family to think of her return.

Besides, he had not expected to see her again so soon. She had said before Christmas that she was only up in London to do some shopping. He had enjoyed a fabulous Christmas. He had always loved Christmas. His father had made it a magical time for him growing up, and he was determined to make it just as special for his daughter Lydia. He had watched Lydia opening her stocking excitedly at some ungodly hour. He had not minded. Being woken at the crack of dawn was all part of the joy of being a dad. Wonderful cooking smells had wafted through the entire house all day. The three of them had eaten a delicious breakfast together then they had all trundled down to cause mayhem with his father and Marlayna. Carrie had stayed over of course. He and Sarah had played with Lydia and her new toys. He had enjoyed all the fantastic food and then spent a lazy afternoon with everyone chatting and watching a bit of telly. Then when they were all tired after all that food, he had carried Lydia upstairs after she had kissed everyone and put her to bed. She had protested that she wasn't at all sleepy, as she always did and then promptly fallen asleep during her nightly Silly Sausage story.

Sarah had been sitting curled up sleepily on the sofa when he tiptoed out of Lydia's bedroom. "Come here gorgeous," he had said smiling down at her with his arms open wide. Sarah had smiled contentedly back at him and reached out toward him. "Mmmmm give me a Christmas kiss please.," she had murmured. "Oh, I think I can just about manage a bit more than a kiss." he had whispered. They had made love by the glow of the twinkling fairy lights. It had been a fantastic day. The news that Jay was now conscious and getting better had perked everyone up.

He had not expected Louise to show her face again anytime soon. When she had popped her head around the door on that first bitterly cold morning in January and said cheerily, "A bit belated, but happy new year!" He had not known how to react. Her presence made him uncomfortable, if he was honest. He felt as if he was being disloyal to Sarah by entertaining another woman. He had meant to tell her as tactfully as possible to cool it, but then she had told him how ill her mother was and he could tell that she had really needed a shoulder to cry on. Jonny had not had the heart to tell her to stop visiting the shop. She had taken to popping in every week now.

She always turned up with lunch and would stay for an hour or so. He made polite conversation with her, and she seemed to leave less troubled. As the weeks had passed, Louise had told him how her mother's health was deteriorating, and how her father seemed to be falling apart at the prospect of losing his beloved wife. Her cancer was inoperable and now they were playing a waiting game. He hated keeping secrets from Sarah, but he knew if he told her about Louise's regular visits to the shop it would cause an argument. Maybe it was time to come clean, though. After all, he had not actually done anything wrong. He made his mind up to confess later at home and then resolutely began to tackle his paper work.

Right on cue, the doorbell tinkled and of course, it was Louise.

Sarah and Suzy had the radio on in the shop. Their January sale was over, and they were now getting ready for Valentine's day. The window display was festooned with cupids, hearts, and romantically themed gift baskets. Penny Chalmers their wonder woman window dresser had worked her usual magic. It was mid-week though and they were hardly rushed off their feet.

"How is Jay feeling now, Suze? I bet he's glad to be home at last." Sarah was putting out more Valentine cards on the shelves. Suzy was behind the counter jiggling to the tune on the radio. It was Dexy's Midnight Runners singing "Come on Eileen"

"He's doing great. He goes back to work after half term. I just wish they would lock up the bastard that did this to him..Oh, I do love this song.." she cranked up the volume and both girls sang along tunelessly . When it finished Suzy turned the volume down a touch and said to Sarah, "It's so quiet today, why don't you give yourself a break and go and have lunch with Jon? You deserve it after holding the fort here for so long. It's about time I pulled my weight again. Give him a ring; I can manage on my own for a bit." Sarah's face lit up.

"Ooh, are you sure? I won't ring him, I'll surprise him. Thanks Suze, I'd love that."

Sarah shivered as she walked along Upper Street. It was a typical grey drizzly February day. There was a biting wind, which blew the icy rain into her face. Roll on spring, she told herself ruefully. She crossed over by the High Pavements, carefully weaving her way through the relentless flow of traffic, and headed into Camden Passage. She had bought a deep pan pizza to share with Jonny. It was their favourite, with extra mushrooms. The box was still nice and warm. Sarah was very grateful for the warmth. She had forgotten her gloves and her fingers were numb with the cold. The pizza smelled delicious and she felt her stomach rumble in anticipation. She was starving. Adam had not joined them today and they had not had their elevenses. It was unusual for him not to pop in, but he had said yesterday that he had a meeting. Sarah realised she looked forward to their daily chats. He was a nice man.

Sarah pushed the door of the shop open and stopped dead in her tracks. Jonny looked up, mortified. He was sitting behind the counter happily sharing lunch with Sarah's old adversary. Louise double barrelled spoiled brat. She was one shadow from the past that Sarah had hoped she would never have to clap eyes on ever again. They looked very cosy together; sitting huddled up with their hands wrapped around mugs of steaming soup. Sarah felt a pain in her heart as if she had been pierced with a rapier.

Louise looked around as the door opened and smiled brightly at Sarah. In a split second, she realised from the expression on Sarah's face that she knew nothing of her renewed friendship with Jonny. So, he had not mentioned her to his dear little wifey. She was delighted. Battle had commenced, and Louise felt she had the upper hand for once.

"Oh, fabulous, have you come to join us for one of our lunches?" she chirped, feigning innocence.

Louise realised she should have kept her mouth shut as soon as the words left her lips. Jonny flashed her a look that was deadly. He knew what she was up to. In an instant, he had rushed from behind the counter and was at Sarah's side.

"Sarah, please, come in, let me explain..." his voice trailed off helplessly as Sarah shoved the pizza box towards him. It left a grease stain on Jonny's crisp white shirt.

"No, don't bother!" she shouted icily. Her eyes flickered towards Jonny's abandoned soup beaker. "I can see you've had your starter. Here's your main course. Enjoy your lunch you two." She turned on her heels and left.

Adele Crayford shivered in the dimly lit room. She wondered how things had escalated so quickly. She had been such a bloody fool. They had enjoyed a lovely Christmas. Martin's mum had made them very welcome and had been really kind to Dennis. Martin had been very subdued all over the holiday, though, and when Adele had asked him what was wrong, he had nearly bitten her head off. She had been shocked, although he had been quick to apologise. He had been loving and attentive and had held her gently in the lumpy old bed in his mother's spare bedroom. He had said he was tired, that was all, and a bit worried about work. Then he had kissed her and made love to her. She had felt so happy. He had given her a beautiful gold necklace on Christmas morning. It was a wonderful surprise. She had not expected such a lavish gift.

Adele had not been suspicious until after Boxing Day when she said it was time to go back home so Dennis could get ready to go back to school. "We're not going back," Martin had said bluntly. Adele had been puzzled, had told him they had to, the social services had insisted, they would get into terrible trouble, and anyway, what about work? "Stuff work, stuff them all!" Martin had replied, red in the face.

"Martin, what's got into you? What's going on?" it was then that Adele felt the first prickling of fear.

She had argued, of course. She had told Martin that she was going back and was taking Dennis. Defiantly she said that Martin could stay if he wanted to, but she had to get back. He had grabbed her arms then. She had heard Dennis screaming in fear, and felt her own heart pounding as her husband's hot breath close to her ear whispered menacingly, "You ain't going nowhere darling. Not without me, anyway."

Adele had had no choice but to comply. She had done her best at the time to placate Martin. His grip on her arms had felt like a vice. It had left bruises that lasted for weeks. He had not hit her, not then, but she was afraid. Every time she saw the livid bruises on her arms, she was reminded of what he was capable of. She knew that something was very wrong and she had to find out what it was.

It was a week into the New Year before she managed to slip out. She waited until Martin was asleep and slipped her coat over her pyjamas.

91

She ran quietly to the phone box on the corner of the street and called her mother. "My God, Adele, where have you been? I've had the police and the social round here looking for you!" Adele listened to her mother open mouthed. Her mother ranted for quite some time. Martin was wanted for a serious assault. He had lied to her. He had not had a fight in a pub as he had told her, he had actually assaulted Dennis's teacher, Jay Oakland. She felt sick. She also felt ashamed. Jay Oakland was such a lovely man. Dennis adored him. No wonder Martin did not want to go back and face the music.

She never should have confronted him when she got back, but she had been so angry. She had only wanted to reason with him, make him realise that running away was not the answer. She had still believed that he was a decent man at heart, that he would do the right thing. Especially now she knew the truth. It was when she saw the fear on his own mother's face that she realised how stupid she had been. All the shouting had woken her and Dennis up of course. His mother had sat crying on the sofa, with poor terrified Dennis rocking back and forth beside her. "Martin" his mother had whispered from the corner of the sofa, "Son, have you been taking your medication?"

"I don't need any bloody pills!" Martin had spat out furiously.

"You know what the doctors said!" his mother had cried desperately. Martin had not replied. He had simply loomed over his poor cowering mother and slapped her across the face.

Now she and Dennis were prisoners. He had dragged her and Dennis screaming to the car in the middle of the night. They were still in their pyjamas. He had left his mother behind, sobbing into the darkness as he drove them away. Adele had been too afraid to ask about the medication, or why he was supposed to take it.

They were now in some semi derelict God forsaken chalet on a holiday camp in Jaywick Sands, of all places. It was freezing and deserted. Most of the chalets in this part of the camp looked neglected. Some had builders hoardings up outside, indicating that repair work was about to be undertaken. The weather now was so cold and wet that work had not yet begun. Martin kept them locked inside. He had been gone for hours. When he went out, he tied her and Dennis to the rickety chairs that were around the worn dark wood dining table. It was useless shouting. There was no one close by to hear. Adele had lost count of how long they had been kept captive.

 Dennis was by her side, whimpering pitifully. "Can we go home soon mum?" he said between sobs. Adele tried to soothe her son. She felt so guilty.it was all her fault that they were here now. She had been such an idiot. The rope around her wrists had made her hands numb and she could not move. She was bursting for the toilet and her stomach was groaning with hunger. Dennis had not had his epilepsy medication since they had been here and she was terrified he would fit again and hurt himself. Last night's seizure had gone on for what seemed like an eternity. Martin had been pitiless however. She had begged him to get help but he had ignored her pleas, as he always did.

"Shhh darling. Please try to be quiet," Adele whispered desperately to Dennis. "You know how it makes Martin angry when you cry. He might be back at any minute. Mummy will try and get us away as soon as I can."

Jonny dropped the pizza box on the shop floor and shouted to Sarah to come back. She ignored him and hurried along Camden passage. "Louise, you have to go. Now!" Jonny's face was set in anger and Louise tried to make things better. "Surely you should leave her, let her calm down a bit" she wheedled. Jonny ushered her to the door. "Just go, Louise, I'm sorry, but I haven't got time for you right now. I have to go after Sarah."

Sarah blinked back her tears and rushed as fast as she could away from the shop. She ignored the angry horns of the traffic as she dodged across the road back to the high pavement of Upper Street. The icy rain was falling heavier now; it felt like a million needles pricking her skin. The trees that lined the edges of the high pavement had to bend and yield to avoid having their limbs ripped out by the cruel gusts of wind. Sarah tried to wipe her hair out of her eyes. She was not looking where she was going. "Heh! Slow down!" said a familiar voice. It was Adam Sandford. Sarah had almost bumped into him. "Sorry" she said tearfully, hanging her head. Her hair was dancing wildly in the wind, and she quietly tried in vain to tame it. He saw her tear stained face and cold nose and said with genuine concern "Are you alright? Sarah, what is it?"

Sarah was embarrassed now. "It's nothing. I'm fine, honest. I..I'm just on my way back to the shop"

"You are not fine; for one thing you look frozen. Your hair needs calming down and so do you, by the look on your face. Have you had lunch? I'm just going to grab a bite after my meeting. Come on; let me get you a drink."

Before she could protest, Adam had steered her into The Passage pub. A glorious waft of warm air met them as the door opened and Sarah sunk gratefully into a chair. Adam sat opposite her and unbuttoned his overcoat. "Okay, I'm not going anywhere until you tell me what's up, now spill. What the hell is wrong?"

"I shouldn't be boring you with my problems," Sarah said, looking even more embarrassed.

"Right. I'm going to get you a drink. You look like you've never needed one more." Sarah opened her mouth to protest, but Adam put his hand up to silence her. He smiled gently and added, "And don't give me any guff about not drinking at lunchtime. I'm your market inspector, and this is purely medicinal. Have you had lunch? You didn't answer when I asked you earlier. Too busy trying to get your barnet to behave." Sarah thought of the lovely wasted pizza. She shook her head. "I'll get us something then. I'm starving. What do you fancy?"

Jonny looked up and down the high street frantically. Sarah had disappeared into thin air. He headed for the little shop in Chapel Market, hoping she had made her way back to work. He was soaked now, and shivering. He had rushed out without his coat. By the time he pushed open the door, a surprised Suzy looked up and saw a bedraggled Jonny looking almost blue with cold.

"Jon? What are you doing here? Where's Sarah?"

"I was hoping she was here with you. Have you seen her?" Suzy shook her head, a worried expression appearing on her face. "Come in, you look half dead. What the hell has happened?"

Sarah felt much better after a large vodka and tonic and a plate of pie and chips. The pub grub was surprisingly good. Slowly, between mouthfuls, she told Adam all about it. She felt like an idiot now she had calmed down. Maybe she had over reacted. Adam had listened quietly.

After he swallowed his last forkful of pie, he leaned back in his chair slightly and said, "Do you think there is any funny business going on between them?" Sarah said quickly "No, I trust Jon" She had been to the ladies room while Adam ordered their lunch and had managed to drag a comb through her unruly red tresses.

"Well then," Adam prompted gently, "There's no real problem, is there? Tell that Louise to do one, and kiss and make up with Jon." Sarah had to smile. Blokes were so simplistic in their reasoning. Said aloud, it sounded so easy. Why did she still feel so murderous though?

"I know what you're saying makes sense, but.. well, it's the fact that she has obviously been going in for lunch for a while, and Jon kept it secret. He knows how I feel about that little cow. She has always managed to get under my skin. Jon knows that. He should have told me she was back on the scene. We don't keep secrets from one another."

"I'd give him a break if I was you. He obviously kept it secret cos he knew you'd react like this. Blokes just want an easy life. Go easy on him when you see him. It'll all come out in the wash, I promise you." Sarah speared her last chip. "I hope you're right. Thanks for listening Adam. You're a great mate." Adam smiled and winked. His heart still turned over when he looked at Sarah. He thought of Nina and felt a pang of guilt. What did that mean he wondered? He wanted to scoop Sarah in his arms and kiss her tears away. Instead, he smiled and said jovially, "Any time, hun. Marjorie Proops has got nothing on me sweetheart. Fancy another drink before we face the elements again?"

"Oh, go on then."

Jonny had almost run back to the shop. He had hoped Sarah would be waiting there but of course, she was not. He had asked Suzy to get her to ring him immediately if she showed up. He was wet through and tried to dry himself with the small hand towel he kept in the little toilet at the back of the shop. It did not do much good and he made himself a cup of tea to try to warm himself up. While he was out the back, he heard the shop bell tinkle. He sighed heavily. He was not up to facing customers just yet. He put the spoon down and came out with a smile though. Ever the professional, he thought bitterly. A bent figure was picking up squashed pizza from the floor. In his haste to thaw out from the cold, he had forgotten about it. The figure stood up.

It was Sarah. Jonny smiled with relief. Sarah put the squashed pizza box on to the counter and smiled at her very wind swept husband. His shirt was sticking to his skin, and his hair was standing up in damp spikes. "Okay Jon Mason, you had better explain yourself, and if you ever keep secrets from me again, I swear, I'll skin you alive!".

CHAPTER EIGHT

"Are there any biscuits left? I'm famished!" Sarah said to Suzy. It was a grey afternoon in March and the shop had been quiet all day. Suzy had put the kettle on for a cuppa merely to break the monotony. Suzy popped her head round from the little back room, with the biscuit barrel in her hand. "There are only fig rolls left. We don't have any dunking biccies. We ate all the choccy chip ones yesterday."
"Oh, great, give em ere. I love fig rolls."
"Since when? I thought you hated them, you usually tell me off for buying fig rolls." Suzy said incredulously, handing over the biscuits. Sarah took a greedy bite out of one. "I can't get enough of em just lately." She said between munches. "I bought four packets when I did my shopping last week"
Suzy looked at Sarah, and Sarah stopped in her tracks mid chomp. "Oh lor, you're not?" Suzy said, not having to finish the sentence. Sarah swallowed hard. Then she grinned. "You know, now I come to think of it, I might be." She looked a bit sheepish. "well, Jonny had a lot of making up to do after miss posh pants turned up again.." her voice trailed off, then she said happily "Oh blimey mate, I think I could be... the last time I had fig rolls was when I was carrying Lydia.. I think I'm pregnant!"

Adele watched Dennis nervously. He had started rocking again. Adele knew how much this habit of his annoyed Martin. He always rocked incessantly backwards and forwards when he was stressed. It had driven her bonkers when he was younger. She had tried everything to stop him, but nothing had worked until he had gone to Bonny Ridge School. He had stopped for a while when he had gone into Jay Oakland's class. He had been much calmer. Mr Oakland had been so good for Dennis, such a good teacher. Dennis came home from school happy each afternoon and had made so much progress. The rocking stopped and he had had far less tantrums. Adele had been so grateful.
The rocking had begun again when she had met Martin. She had not made the connection until now. She was so stressed herself that she felt

like rocking too. She did not know exactly how long Martin had kept them in this shabby freezing little chalet. It felt like months but was probably only a few weeks. She had begged him to allow them back to their flat, but he had told her not to be stupid, it was out of the question. She had tried asking him to at least go back for Dennis's medication. Once again, he had refused, saying it was too risky; the police were looking for him. "What do you intend doing with us?" she had asked quietly in desperation, fearing the answer. Martin had said nothing. Adele felt she no longer knew the man in front of her. His behaviour had become more and more bizarre. He was talking to himself. It was as if he held conversations with an invisible man. It terrified her. As the days had turned into weeks, she knew he had slipped so far away from her he was beyond reach. His eyes were dead and Adele tried not to panic. She had to remain calm, try to placate him, humour him, to stop Dennis from getting too upset. She tried to keep things as normal as possible but every day she looked for any way to escape. So far, it had been impossible. Martin may have lost his mind, but he was vigilant, and he watched the pair of them all the time. She realised he was very sick, and extremely volatile and she wanted this whole nightmare to be over.

Adele realised that very soon now the holiday camp would be opening up for the Easter and summer season. Martin would have to move them on somewhere else. There was a grounds man who patrolled the campsite every day now, and work had begun on some of the chalets that had needed updating. She had heard Martin speaking to the workmen once or twice. The grounds man had informed Martin that he was not allowed to live in the chalet. He had come in moaning about him after that conversation, calling him a nosy interfering old bastard, but he had moved their car and fobbed the man off, telling him he was sorry for any inconvenience, he was only doing some maintenance to the old chalet before the season began. He had threatened Adele and Dennis and ordered them both not to make a sound. Poor Dennis had been so terrified he had wet himself again. Before he had started school at Bonny Ridge Dennis had often forgotten himself and had toilet accidents. He had stopped for a while when he had settled down at school, but since Martin had come into their lives he had regressed. Once again, Adele cursed herself. Why had she not noticed all the signs

98

of distress in her beloved little boy? She really had been a selfish bitch. Adele had silently cleaned him up and hugged him to her. She tried to reassure her son as best she could, telling him it did not matter. Dennis did not look convinced.

Martin had brought them a change of clothes and food. It was not much but anything was better than nothing at all. He would go out for hours each day though and leave them both bound and gagged on the grimy sofa. He had now covered the seat cushions with plastic sheeting, as Dennis could not control his bladder for the length of time he was left tied up. Martin had said he had to gag them as he could not trust them to stay quiet with the grounds man snooping around. He had spoken to them in a calm, almost soothing voice, as if what he was doing was perfectly normal and acceptable. Adele was frantic now. They were being held hostage and all she could think of was getting Dennis away to safety. She felt so guilty for putting her poor little boy in such danger. She was terrified he would have a seizure and choke to death with the horrible gag over his mouth. Every day she tried desperately to free her bonds so they could escape, but she could not do it. She only succeeded in rubbing her skin raw in trying.

When they heard the sound of Martin's footsteps on the gravel path outside they both exchanged anxious glances. Fear was always mixed with relief. It was so good to be untethered, yet each knew that one wrong move could send Martin into a rage.

He would untie them and expect Adele to cook a meal with the meagre food he brought home. Adele never asked where he got the money to pay for it, or if he stole it. He had said he had not used any cash machines for fear the police would trace his movements. Adele would clean Dennis up, put him in dry clothes, and then begin cooking. As Martin was beginning to stay away for longer and longer periods, she sometimes had to suffer the indignity of cleaning herself up too. Dennis would sit on the floor nervously rocking as Adele cooked. Martin looked over at Dennis in distain. "Can't you stop him doing that?" he said through gritted teeth. Dennis rocked harder. Martin turned his attention back to the television screen as Adele touched Dennis lightly on his shoulder and said, "Dennis darling, why don't you come and help mummy with the cooking? You like helping me, don't you?" Adele smiled reassuringly at her son, hoping he would not detect the desperation in her voice. She flashed her eyes at Dennis and inclined her head towards the kitchen area. She had plenty of time while Martin was out to think of ways to escape, but so far, it had been impossible. When Martin was around he never took his eyes off her for a second. This evening however, he was engrossed in the television. He loved football and a big match was about to begin.

Obediently, Dennis stood up and walked towards the kitchen cupboards. Martin switched channels on the television. He did not allow them to watch television unless he was with them. He did not want them hearing on the news that the police were still looking for them. He wanted to watch football this evening though. He put his feet up on the battered old coffee table and sipped one of the cans of lager he had brought in as the theme music for match of the day began. He did not usually sit with his back to Adele, but this was the best position to see the screen. He had tried moving the television set, but the reception was not good and no matter how much he swore and fiddled with the ariel, the television only got a half decent picture in this position. He soon became focused on the game. Arsenal was playing their old adversaries Spurs. "Come on, shoot you moron!" Martin said, never taking his eyes from the flickering TV set. Adele watched him as she clanked noisily at the stove. She knew that Martin would not turn around so long as he could hear her cooking in the background, not while Arsenal was playing. This game was a very important match. He was obsessed.

"Pass me that frying pan would you Dennis?" she said a little too loudly. "No, that's a saucepan. That's it, good boy, the one next to it. We can cook the sausages. Do you want to sing? Two fat sausages, sizzling in a pan..."

Dennis held the heavy pan in both his hands. He looked at his mother. She was staring at Dennis, but still singing quietly. "One went pop and the other went bang."

Dennis glanced nervously over at his loathsome stepfather. He could just see the back of his head over the top of the grubby sofa. Martin was leaning forward watching the game intently. Dennis looked pleadingly back at his mother, and his eyes flickered to the pan in his hands. In an instant, Adele realised Dennis understood. She had been wondering if she dared take the chance. It could be now or never. She nodded. Dennis silently handed the pan to his mother.

Adele had never moved so quietly, or with such stealth. "That's it Dennis, good boy. You like helping me, don't you?" she said encouragingly. Adele put her finger to her lips and hoped that Dennis would remain silent. She inched towards Martin, the heavy frying pan raised above his head. Then she swung the pan like a cricket bat with all her might until it connected with her husband's skull.

The clunk as the pan hit Martin's head was worthy of a Tom and Jerry cartoon episode. Adele almost expected stars to appear in the air. The impact sent a shooting pain through Adele's wrists and she dropped the pan .Martin slumped to one side, out cold. The pan fell with a dull thud and it clunked onto the floor.

Adele grabbed Dennis by the hand and together they fled into the night.

Sarah had stopped off at Boots the chemist on her way home from work and bought a pregnancy test. She would not tell Jonny until she was certain. If the test was positive, she planned a nice romantic meal, and she would tell him then. She hoped he would be thrilled. Things were still a bit fraught at home. They were both trying very hard, but Sarah still felt that Jonny was hiding something. It was not like him, and Sarah did not like it at all.

Carrie felt her chest tightening and she tried not to panic. As the pain radiated outward and spread down her arm, she reached for her telephone. She was sweating and struggling to remain calm as she dialled 999.

Sarah called Jon in a panic, and he closed the shop and came at once. Carrie had been rushed to hospital with a suspected heart attack. The doctor in A&E told them that Carrie had already been taken up to the ward. She was sleeping.

A nurse ushered Sarah and Jonny to Carrie's bedside. She had been made comfortable in a room on her own by the nurse's station in acute care. Sarah had broken down in floods of tears seeing her mother wired up to all sorts of equipment. The nurses had tried to reassure her, and she had tried her best to calm down.

Suzy arrived as soon as she could. Tearfully she hugged Sarah. "I thought you would have seen enough of hospitals to last you a life time." Sarah managed to say through her own tears as she pulled away from her friend. She was so pleased to see her though. "Don't be daft," Suzy said, attempting a weak smile, "You know I'll always be here whenever you need me. Blimey mate, just when we thought things were settling down, eh? How is she?" Sarah could not speak. The tears were spilling down her cheeks again. She just shrugged her shoulders. Jonny helped her out. "The doctors say she's stable. They will know more in a few days." He handed Sarah a clean tissue.
"Well, don't worry about the shop, or Lyddy. You know we'll all pitch in. Mum has already volunteered, and I know Marlayna and Vick will be there. Just look after your mum." Suzy said as cheerfully as she could manage.

Carrie drifted in and out of consciousness after the surgery to repair her heart valve. Sarah sat loyally by her bedside and stroked the back of her hand. She was still choked up as Carrie had told her she knew she was going to die. "You can't know that!" Sarah had said desperately. "You don't know what you are saying. That's just the medication talking! The doctors said there's no reason you shouldn't make a full recovery. I don't want you thinking things like that." Carrie opened her eyes and looked at her daughter. She smiled at her sadly. "Sarah, it's okay, really it is. You know, I have had such a good life since...well, since your dad.. is not around anymore. It's been like a dream. I'm free. I never knew how good it could be Sarah love, not being afraid. I want you to promise me something, though." Sarah nodded. She could not speak. She had a lump in her throat the size of a boulder. Her mother had not spoken about her father in a very long time. It was too painful for both of them.
"I want you to tell Jonny." Carrie said urgently, gripping tightly onto Sarah's sleeve. Sarah shifted in her hard plastic chair uncomfortably. "Tell him what?" she whispered, although she knew only too well what her mother meant.
"Please Sarah," Carrie whispered, looking desperately at her daughter, "Don't keep our secret from Jonny any longer. It will eat you up eventually, as it has done to me. I have never got over it, Sarah. I don't

102

want it doing that to you. He needs to know the truth. Promise me you will tell Jonny. No more secrets, promise me!"

"Tell me what?" Jonny said. He had left the room to go to the vending machine for coffee. He stood there in the doorway with a puzzled look on his face and two polystyrene cups in his hand.

Sarah sat opposite Jonny in their living room. They had come home to try to get some rest, although Sarah knew she would not be able to sleep, even though she felt absolutely exhausted. Lydia was spending the night downstairs with Victor and Marlayna. Jonny had come upstairs after telling Lydia her bedtime story and had pressed Sarah to tell him what Carrie had meant. Sarah had tried to fob him off, but Jonny would not let it drop.

Sarah found it difficult to find the right words, and it had taken her a long time to try to explain. Eventually, she had begun, and once she started, the whole story had tumbled out of her mouth. She did not look at Jonny. She had found it strangely cathartic to unburden herself. It was such a relief to finally share the terrible secret she had carried around for such a long time. Eventually she stopped talking and looked at Jonny. She bit her lip in horror as she saw the expression on his face.

He sat in stunned silence, a look of disbelief creasing his handsome features. She had hoped he would pull her close to him, tell her he understood, that everything would be all right. She needed his support so badly, especially now, with her mother critically ill in hospital. Looking at Jonny's face, she had never felt so alone.

Sarah had come home to find Carrie that terrible night in deep shock after giving her husband Tommy a massive, fatal insulin dose. Sarah had taken charge, telling her mother that they would keep what she had done to themselves. The death certificate had been recorded as accidental death. Tommy had been drinking heavily that night and he was usually very insistent on doing his own insulin injections. It was believed that in his drunken state; he had accidently given himself the wrong dosage. The silence in the room was palpable as Jonny digested what Sarah had finally told him.

Eventually Jonny said, "That is one hell of a secret to keep from me."

103

The row had quickly spiralled out of control. They had both shouted and Sarah had lost her temper and hurled a cup across the room. It had landed with an almighty crash as it hit the door. Tea dripped down the woodwork and Sarah stood panting, with her fists clenched in fury and frustration. Sarah realised that Jon just could not understand. How could he? His world had always been one of cosy kindness, and love. Victor would never lay a finger on Jonny. He had always spoiled him, in the nicest possible way, but Jonny was quite naïve regarding the harsher realities of life. Sarah envied him. Despite growing up without his mother, he had experienced an idyllic childhood. Victor had always been there to support him, with love understanding and tenderness. Sarah had only known love from her mother. She had witnessed nothing but brutality from her father and they had lived in fear and trepidation every single day. She knew what her mother had done was wrong in the eyes of the law, but she needed to convey to Jonny the desperation that had driven her to take such drastic measures. She had tried, but he simply was not listening. Sheer frustration made her livid with anger.

Jon looked at the tea dripping and then at Sarah. "I think I need time to cool off." He said quietly. "I had better go. I just can't believe you and your mum did such a thing. It..it's so horrible. It was...murder, for God's sake! Not only that, but you kept it from me all this time. After all you said about keeping secrets. It's so hypocritical, Sarah." Before Sarah had a chance to reply, Jon slammed out of the flat.

"Don't you dare leave me like this!" Sarah screamed furiously. Then she added in desperation, a sob escaping from her mouth, "Please don't leave me all alone!"

It was too late. Jonny had already gone.

Once out in the street, Jonny realised he had no idea where to go, but he really needed a drink.

Sarah tried her best to calm down after Jonny left. She made herself another cup of tea and switched on the television, but she could not settle. She had to talk to someone, so she rang Suzy.

"Oh Suze, I'm sorry, I didn't expect you to come tearing round." Twenty minutes after Sarah's frantic garbling down the phone, Suzy had turned up at the flat. Victor and Marlayna were keeping a discrete distance downstairs, but obviously knew something was seriously amiss. They had heard the shouting and then Jonny slamming out of the front door. Sarah was very grateful that they did not try to interfere. "I was worried about you, you daft cow" Suzy said pleasantly, "Now, get me a drink and tell me all. I couldn't make head nor tail of what you said down the phone. I gather you and Jon have had a massive barny, but that's about it." Sarah felt her cheeks burning. She should have kept her mouth shut. "It's..nothing, really" she mumbled, going into the kitchen to try to find something alcoholic for Suzy to drink. Suzy was not going to be fobbed off so easily. She actually grabbed Sarah by the shoulder and forced her to look directly at her. "Now look," she said in her firmest voice, "I haven't dragged myself away from my hot husband and a good night's telly for nothing. I know something serious is up, and I ain't moving until you tell me. So spill! I know you had a row, but for gawds sake, what is going on?" To Suzy's surprise, Sarah burst into tears.

It took Sarah a long time to tell Suzy. She had been so afraid that her dearest friend would react just as Jonny had. Even worse, she was terrified that Suzy would be horrified, and their friendship would be ruined. She knew that she could not lie to her friend however. Maybe it was time to share the heavy burden she had guarded for so long. She took a deep breath and began.

Suzy sat quietly and let Sarah talk without interrupting. When Sarah eventually fell silent, she put her arms around Sarah. Sarah sobbed with relief. "It's all okay, don't cry anymore" Suzy said, herself choking back tears. She looked at her friend's blotchy face and managed a little smile. "I don't know how you kept that to yourself all this time," she said softly.

"I...I.. was so afraid that you would hate me, and I didn't want me or my mum to go to prison." Sarah said between sobs. "You don't hate me, do you?" she added desperately. Suzy hugged her again.

"Hate you? You daft old bat, of course I don't hate you! I admire your courage! Your poor mum, she must have gone through hell. You know, looking back over our childhood, I can't ever remember a time when your mum wasn't covered in bruises. I can't imagine what your lives were like. I tell you, I would have killed that wicked old bastard a long time ago if I'd been you!"

Sarah laughed in relief. "I wish Jonny could be as broad minded as you." Sarah said after sipping her tea. It had grown cold while she talked, and she pulled a face and got up to make a fresh cup.

"Oh, he'll come round, you'll see. Your Jonny has always put you on a pedestal you know that. Finding out that you are human must have been a hell of a shock for him."

Sarah made more tea and topped up Suzy's wine glass. "Will you tell your mum and dad?" Sarah asked Suzy eventually. Suzy shook her head. "Not if you don't want me to." She said gently, sipping her wine. "Besides, I have a hunch they have always suspected anyway." Sarah's eyes widened in shock, and Suzy couldn't help smiling. "Don't worry, hun, they love your mum and you as much as I do. We will always be here for you."

Jonny had gone off in such a rage he had no clear plan of what he was going to do or where he was going. He was not much of a drinker normally, but he felt he had never needed an alcoholic prop more. He headed for Serendipity's. This was a wine bar above the shopping arcade in Camden passage. He knew the bar manager, Jeff. He had not seen Jeff for years until a few weeks ago. He had bumped into him in Camden Passage and Jeff had told him he had landed a bar managers job in the wine bar. Jonny had promised to drop in one day. Sarah did not like it in there much; she had described it as a bit poncy, full of yuppy types in suits and posh accents. All the more reason to go there then, he had fumed.

It was busy. He saw Jeff dashing from customer to customer as the noise and chatter hit him. He had not even had much time to chat with Jeff, who had been rushed off his feet all night. Jeff had been an old school friend. They both shared an interest in classic cars. It was a shame he was so busy now. A friendly chat about cars would have helped calm him down.

He had not spotted Louise at first. He had pushed his way to the bar and ordered a double vodka downing it in one and ordered another. Jeff had raised his eyebrows. "Rough day?" he had said grinning. Jonny nodded grimly. "Oh yeah. The kind of day that makes me want to get very, very drunk!" He slammed his glass down on the counter, and told

Jeff to top it up again. "You'll regret it in the morning," Jeff said sagely as he poured.

"I'm sure I will." Jonny said, swallowing his vodka, "But right now I don't much care"

Louise had sidled over, and Jonny looked at her in surprise. She was the last person he wanted or expected to see. "Please leave me alone." Jonny had said coldly, "I'm in no mood for company, especially your company." He did not see her leave; he was not sure what happened to her or her friend who he vaguely remembered lurking in Louise's shadow.

He did not remember anything much after that. All he remembered was waking up with a throbbing head and a mouth that felt like the bottom of a budgies cage.

It took a while for him to realise that he was naked and in Louise's bed.

Louise felt numb. She had been with her father all night at her mother's hospital bedside. Her mother had passed away in the early hours and she sat now, in the family living room trying to comfort her distraught father. They had just arrived home. The sun was beginning to rise and Louise had managed to persuade her father to leave the hospital. Her father had not wanted to leave his wife's bedside. Louise had had to endure her mother's rapid decline over the last few weeks. The cancer had been relentless. It had spread into her liver and then on to her brain. She had been admitted to hospital once it reached her liver. She had been in a coma for three days before slipping away. Louise had made her father a cup of coffee which was left untouched on the table beside his favourite armchair. Louise sat on the floor beside him and held his hand as he stared wordlessly into space. He was in deep shock. Eventually she told her father that she needed to use the bathroom. She made her excuses and went to splash cold water on her blotchy tear stained face. She went into her bedroom after drying her face. She sat on her bed. She ached inside and felt so alone. She opened her handbag and took out the photograph of a naked Jonny. Keeping it in her bag, close to her at all times was somehow comforting. She felt as if she had a lucky talisman with her. She kissed the photo and longed for Jonny. Another tear spilled down her cheek and she bit her lip. Eventually she dried her eyes. She carefully tucked the photograph back into her bag.

He had been sleeping when she had taken the photograph, of course. Well, he had passed out. He knew nothing about the photograph; he had been dead to the world.

She had been incredibly hurt when he had been so rude to her in the wine bar. She had been so thrilled when he had walked in. Camilla had been late, and Louise had been nursing a large glass of Chardonay alone in a corner. She had arranged to meet Camilla here, as she always lived in hope of spotting Jonny. He worked so close by; she thought he might walk past one time. She always tried to sit at a table near the window. She could just see where Jonny worked from the window seat. So far, she had never seen him, but her luck had finally changed. Camilla had wanted to tell her something. She had rung Louise earlier. Louise had been glad for an excuse to escape the hospital for a few hours.

Louise nearly missed Camilla once Jonny arrived. She had switched her gaze from the door to the bar, never letting Jonny out of sight. Her flustered friend had eventually appeared in front of her. She had wanted to go somewhere else, stressed again that she had said she needed to speak to her, and it was too noisy in here. Louise had not wanted to leave, of course. Was Camilla mad? In the end, Camilla had sat down resignedly and poured herself a large glass of wine from the bottle in front of Louise. She had let Camilla rattle on, but Louise had not really been listening. She had kept her eyes firmly on Jonny. He had staggered out side at closing time and Louise had seen him swaying slightly on the pavement. She had stepped off the kerb and hailed a taxi, bundling Jonny into it. Camilla had looked outraged when she had climbed in beside him. "Oh don't look so miffed!" she had said dismissively to Camilla, leaning out of the cab. "I'll ring you tomorrow. There's bound to be another cab along in a minute." With that, she had slammed the cab door shut. The cab had pulled away, leaving Camilla behind.

Jonny had passed out in the cab. She had had to bribe the taxi driver to help her carry him across the Barbican concourse and up to her flat. She had managed to put him to bed. She had not been able to resist taking his clothes off and tucking him up lovingly. She had admired his well-toned body and on impulse had pulled back the covers again and taken the snapshot. She had lain beside him, watching his breathing for a long time before eventually falling asleep herself.

She got up and wearily returned to her father's side. He looked up at her, more composed now. "I expect you'll want to ring Rupert and let him know." He said quietly, automatically. "You'll need his support at a time like this." Louise nodded. She could not trust herself to speak. Her husband had not even entered her thoughts until that moment.

Carrie had made a remarkable recovery after her operation. She had undergone surgery to repair the defective heart valve, but was now looking much more like her old self. Sarah had been to see her before they took her down to the theatre and had whispered "Mum, you have to get well. You have so much to live for. I haven't told anyone else yet, not even Jonny, but I'm expecting another baby. You have another grandchild to look forward to meeting." Carrie had squeezed Sarah's hand and smiled in delight. She had blown Sarah a kiss as she was wheeled into the operating room.

The nurses had her up a few days after her operation and she had gained her strength back slowly. As she recovered, she felt foolish for getting maudlin and telling Sarah that she thought she was going to die. Sarah had just laughed, and told her sheepish looking mother that it did not matter. Sarah was overjoyed that Carrie was doing so well. She patted her mother's hand and said conspiratorially, "Don't forget, we have another wonderful little secret now. Lydia and the new baby both need their Nana."

Sarah had been so distraught she had forgotten all about the pregnancy test that she had bought. She had not even mentioned it to Jon. She had not forgiven him for leaving her when she had been so upset, or for staying out all night. She had longed for Jonny to hold her and tell her that everything would be all right, but he had left her just when she needed him most. He had done nothing but apologise since slinking back shame faced the following morning. He had told her he got blind drunk and crashed out at his friend Jeff's place. Sarah had maintained a stony silence, despite Jonny's attempts to make things right. Things were frosty in the Mason household. Sarah put on a brave face and sat beside Carrie's bed. She held her mums arm as Carrie slowly went for little walks along the hospital corridor. The nurses said it was important to build up her strength and prevent blood clots forming. They had advised Carrie about her diet, and worked out a gentle exercise plan for her to continue her recovery. Sarah did not want Carrie to realise that things were not good at home; she knew her mum would blame herself. The last thing she needed right now was more stress.

The doctors had finally told Carrie she could go home the next day, so long as she rested and did not over do things, and stuck to her healthy living diet.

"That is fantastic news!" Suzy said, smiling at Sarah who had popped into the shop to tell her the good news about her mum. "Maybe we can all get back to normal now. Talking of which, have you told him yet?" Sarah's cheeks reddened. She had finally done the pregnancy test and it had been positive. It had only confirmed what she already knew. As well as her fig roll craving she had been sick every day for the past month. Now it was official however, she felt she had to tell someone, so she had told Suzy. "Um..no. I told my mum I was pregnant before her op. I thought it would give her something to hang on to. I just can't bring myself to tell Jonny. I haven't forgiven him for staying out all night and leaving me when I needed him. I was so worried about my mum, and he buggered off. I felt so let down, Suze. I never expected Jon to let me down." She could not help it, she felt her voice crack as she spoke, and her eyes swam with tears. Maybe it was her hormones going crazy she told herself but everything seemed to make her tearful right now. Suzy stroked Sarah's arm soothingly.

"I know, but he's only human, Ra. Cut him some slack. He'll be thrilled about the baby. Don't tell him you told your mum or me first, either. Men get upset about that sort of thing." She grinned. "Go on, make it up. You know you want to, you're lost without him. Put on your sexiest frock, make him something special to eat and make his bloody day!"

Jonny opened the front door and saw the pink rose petals trailing up the stairs towards the flat. Sarah had also placed little tea lights in coloured glass holders on each step to guide his way. He grinned, closed the street door as quietly as he could and raced up the stairs. The smell of a beef casserole filled his nostrils as he opened the door to their flat and his stomach groaned in appreciation. Jonny usually did most of the cooking. He was an accomplished cook, but since Lydia had been born, Sarah had learned how to cook a few dishes exceptionally well. Her beef casserole was one of her specialities. The table was set for dinner for two and Sarah was sitting at the table expectantly. She looked beautiful. She was wearing her favourite jade green dress that he always found irresistible, and her hair was like spun copper cascading around her shoulders. Her smile lit up her face as he came into the room. She lit the candles on the table and said "Dinner is ready. Come and sit down. I've got some good news to tell you."

Much later, as Sarah relaxed in a nice warm bubble bath, Jonny kneeled beside her and gently washed her back. He kissed her shoulder fondly. She turned to him. "Jon, we are all right, aren't we?"
"Oh sweetheart, of course we are!" he said urgently. "I told you when I first met you; you are in my heart and in my blood. You always will be. I know I can be a silly bugger at times, but please, don't ever doubt how much I love you. I was bloody stupid, a complete moron. I have had plenty of time to mull things over, and I realise I have no idea what it was like for you and your mum. I tried my best to imagine, I spoke to my dad and he gave me a good telling off. He said I needed to grow up." Jon grinned sheepishly. "He was right as usual. I am so sorry. I think I would have done exactly the same if I had been in your position. I hope you can forgive me."
Sarah smiled then, and leaned back amongst the bubbles. She closed her eyes reliving the sensations of earlier. They had not made it to the bedroom. After their meal when Jon had calmed down after she had told him about the baby, he had seized her around the waist and lifted her onto the dining table. "Mind the candles!" she had giggled.
"Never mind the bloody candles," he had whispered in to her ear. "Lie back and let me show you how much I want you."

Jonny could not stop grinning. He was going to be a father again. Everything was going to be all right. Carries was looking so much more like her old self now. He thought how close they had come to losing her and he had been so thankful to still have her.
 He was ashamed of himself for not being more understanding when he had found out what Carrie had done to her husband. It had been a shock, and he had reacted very badly. He had looked at his mother in laws lovely face and had wondered how anyone could hurt her. Tommy,

her husband and Sarah's father had beaten her mercilessly for years. How any man could resort to such cowardice was beyond his comprehension. He thought he understood now what had driven poor Carrie to take such drastic action. It broke his heart to think of how petrified she and his beautiful Sarah must have been, living with that monster day after day. Tommy had beaten Sarah too. Just thinking about him was making his own blood boil. He could not bear the thought of any one hurting Sarah. He could not stop smiling now though, when he recalled his own dad's face when he and Sarah had told him about the new baby. It had been priceless. Marlayna had danced around the room in delight, and even his darling Lydia had been pleased. She had said with childish honesty that she would prefer a hamster, and after they had all finished laughing she had said, "I don't mind really. Amy says her little brother is not as bad as she thought he'd be. He's a bit of a pest, but Amy likes having him to play with most of the time. I s'pose a baby sister wouldn't be too bad. Will it be a girl, mum?" Sarah had hugged her and said grinning, "Well, we won't know for a while, and we have to take what we're given sweetheart." Lydia pondered this new nugget of information for a little while and then smiled brightly. She stroked Shady's ears. The Labrador was in her usual place, by Lydia's side. The two of them were inseparable. Shady had barked excitedly at the dancing, but had settled down again now. "Well, mum, do you think Shady will like it?" Sarah nodded, and added, "I'm sure Shady will love the new little baby. She loves all of us we are her family. She looks after us all, doesn't she?" Sarah patted Shady's head fondly. The dog looked up adoringly and thumped her tail. Lydia hugged her mother. Then she said craftily, "Can I have a hamster and a new baby mum? I think Shady would like a hamster to play with."
Jonny grinned at the memory as he opened up the shop. He had just sat down behind the counter to open his post when the shop bell above the door tinkled. He looked up and his heart sank. It was Louise.

The police had gone to the chalet as soon as they could after Adele had called them. She had dragged Dennis as fast as she could away from the campsite. The two of them, breathless and dishevelled had crashed into the nearest shop and Adele had garbled to the bewildered shopkeeper what she had done. She was hysterical, and was certain that she had killed her husband.

They sat at the police station wrapped in blankets, gratefully drinking hot chocolate together while they waited for the police to tell them that Martin had been arrested if he was still alive. A doctor had been to see them both. Dennis had at last seen a doctor and been given his medication. They were waiting to be driven to a safe house.

A young police officer finally appeared. Dennis had fallen asleep and Adele was gently smoothing her son's hair. Adele looked up expectantly as the young officer came into the room.

He quietly informed a devastated Adele that the officers had searched the chalet but Martin had gone.

"Please go away." Jonny said curtly before Louise had her foot through the door. He did not even feel a twinge of guilt as he saw her crestfallen expression. She had caused him nothing but trouble and he could not remember a thing about the events leading up to finding himself in her bed. He had only gone into Serendipity's because he knew Jeff Godfrey, the bar manager. They had been at school together. They were good friends once upon a time but had somehow lost touch. He had not seen Jeff for years until they had bumped into one another in Camden Passage a few weeks ago. Jeff had told him he had just landed a new job. It had been great to have an old familiar face working close by. The wine bar was not far from where Jonny worked. He told Jeff he would pop in one day. He never intended it to be so soon, but he had been in such a foul mood that night after finding out Sarah's secret. The wine bar had seemed like a safe refuge to go to and calm down. He had just wanted to sit and have a drink and maybe cool off with a chat with Jeff. He had not spotted Louise lurking in the corner until it was too late. He had ordered a large vodka and tonic and was chatting about cars with Jeff when Louise had crept over and tapped him on the shoulder. He had not been able to believe his bad luck. She had been the last person he wanted to see. He remembered introducing her to Jeff, and the three of them having a polite stilted conversation. Then Louise's friend Camilla had turned up. She was full of apologies for being so late. Jonny had been relieved to see Camilla, thinking Louise would leave him alone now her friend had finally shown up. He had pointedly turned away and tried to continue his conversation with Jeff. However, it had become crowded in the wine bar and Jeff was busy serving drinks to other customers. Jonny had managed to order himself another large drink and hoped Louise would take the hint and shove off. Of course, she did not. She had almost glued herself to his side, with poor Camilla standing like a spare part gormlessly beside her. She had him cornered. He had eventually stood up to leave, but by that time, after downing so many double vodka's on an empty stomach, he had felt a bit light headed. Louise had pushed him back, saying, "Don't leave. Stay a bit longer." He vaguely remembered swaying a little and he had plonked down on his bar stool again. Another drink had appeared in front of him as if by magic. He had recklessly downed it in one. The room had been spinning by that time and he realised he was very pissed. Louise realised it too. She had laughed and said "Why Jonny Mason, you're pickled." She kept buying drinks for him though. He had tried to refuse but she had insisted. He was too far gone to argue and did not have the will to refuse. Downing more alcohol had seemed like a good idea at the time. What a bloody idiot, he thought bitterly. He should have realised that if he gave Loopy Lou an inch she would take a mile. He did not remember much else. What the hell had happened? How had she managed to get rid of Camilla and get him to her flat? He cursed himself for being such an imbecile. He never drank to excess usually. He hated that feeling of being out of control. That was almost worse than the hangover. He had not been that drunk since his university days. Then he and his friends had gone out after classes and become totally pie eyed on cheap cider in the student union bar. He ruefully remembered missing many a day's lectures in his first year. They had never done anything too drastic whilst plastered though. Well, apart from decorating a few corridors with loo paper and puking a fair bit. He had always regretted it after and had certainly never woken up in any ones bed but his own before. He had not been able to keep up the pace of heavy drink binges. He had had to slow down by his second year, and concentrated on his course work. He had had to endure a stern bollocking from his course lecturer too. Maybe he had just grown up a bit. The novelty of feeling like hell after a bender had lost its appeal certainly.

Louise interrupted his thoughts.

"I need to talk to you." Louise said quietly. She did not look well. Jonny sighed. He raked his fingers through his hair.

"Louise what do you want? I would really be grateful if you just left me alone. I don't have anything else to say to you. Whatever happened that night was a terrible mistake. We need to forget about it and move on. If you need to talk to someone, it should be to your husband, not me. Just go, please, and leave me in peace."

"My mother died." Louise said flatly, as if Jonny had not spoken. Jonny was a bit taken aback. There was an awkward silence. Louise starred at the floor. Eventually Jonny said, "I'm sorry. That must be very hard for you. Send my condolences to your father. I still don't know why you're here though." He was aghast when Louise looked up with tears streaming down her face. "Look, Louise, dry your eyes. Here, take this." He fished a clean tissue out of his pocket and handed it to her. She blew her nose noisily. Gently Jonny tried again.

"I really do think you would be better off away from me. I'm sure your husband would be happy to offer you the support you need. He must be missing you. It's him, not me that you should be crying with. I can't give you anything you need. "

To his horror, this made Louise howl loudly. She was actually sobbing now. He knew she wanted him to put his arm around her so she could cry on his shoulder, but he did not want to touch her. Any physical contact could be so easily misconstrued. He had a sudden vision of Sarah appearing and throttling him for having another woman in his arms. Not just any woman, either, but the dreaded Louise. He was beginning to wonder if Louise was deranged or just delusional.

He let Louise cry noisily. He sat squirming while she sobbed in front of him. He just wanted to get rid of her as quickly as possible. His patience had run out with her now. Eventually when her shoulders stopped heaving and she blew her nose again, he said, "Look Louise, I don't know what you want from me. Whatever it is, I can't give it to you, and I don't want to. I don't know what else I can say. There is never going to be anything between us. I've told you that before. I don't mean to hurt you, but I can't offer you anything. I don't know what happened that..that night, but I can't believe anything er, intimate happened between us. You have a husband and I have a wife. A wife that I am happily married to. I would not be unfaithful to Sarah, not in a million years. I love her way too much. I would never betray her like that. We have a beautiful daughter together, and.." he paused not knowing whether he should tell her or not. Then he thought she might take the hint if she knew so he went on, "and we are expecting another baby together."

Louise was so eaten up with jealousy that she almost choked on the bile that rose in her throat. She was so hurt at hearing the news that she instinctively wanted to lash out. She tried to compose herself as best she could and allowed a small tight smile to briefly touch her face. "Well well, you have been busy, haven't you Jonny?" she said icily. "You're wrong Jonny. You were unfaithful to your precious wife. I came to tell you that I am pregnant too. You need to know because you're the father."

CHAPTER NINE

Jay put down the telephone. He could not believe it. The call had been from the Social worker who worked in conjunction with Bonny Ridge. She had though Jay should know that Dennis and his mother Adele had been found safe and well, but Martin Crayford had disappeared.

"There's something else I think you should know, Jay. Martin Crayford's mother finally told the police. Her son was diagnosed ten years ago with paranoid schizophrenia, and he has not been taking his medication."

"Jay? You all right?" Suzy said, concerned as she saw Jay stroke his stubbly chin. It was still early on Sunday morning and Jay had not shaved yet. They were both still in bed. Jay leaned over and kissed Suzy to reassure her. She smiled and said, "Mmmm that's like kissing sandpaper. I quite like it, though. Give us another." Jay obliged, but then leant back. He told her about the phone call. Suzy swore and then looked shiftily towards the bedroom door in case Amy and Bobby Jay had overheard.

Right on cue, Amy and Bobby Jay came hurtling into the bedroom and dived on the bed. Suzy grinned and held out her arms for her morning cuddle. Jay enveloped little Bobby Jay in a big bear hug and smothered his face in kisses. "Morning terror!" he said when he was able to breathe again. Bobby Jay and Amy were now swopping places, and trampling all over the duvet. Once the trampling, kissing and giggles had died down Suzy said, "Right, who wants scrambled eggs for breakfast?" As Jay ate the last of his eggs, he could not stop thinking about the earlier phone conversation. That bastard Crayford had held Dennis and his mother hostage. Poor little Dennis, he must have been terrified. Martin Crayford was psychotic , and he was still on the loose. Jay looked over at his children who were still eating their own breakfasts. Suzy was in the shower. He could hear the water running and Suzy singing. He did not want to worry her unduly, but he was worried that Crayford would come looking for him again. He would not mind betting that someone like Martin Crayford would want to finish what he started or try to get at Jay through the children or Suzy. He would have to tell Suzy his concerns. If the bastard were capable of holding his own wife and stepson hostage, who knew what he would do. He was already on edge. They had new and very antisocial next door neighbours. Old Narky Norris had been taken to hospital after a nasty fall. Word had got round that he would not be able to return to his flat next door for some time. It had been blissfully peaceful for a while, as the flat had remained empty. Jay and Suzy had been surprised when one day a young family had moved in. Suzy had at first welcomed them, and was relieved that a couple with young children were living next door. She had soon changed her mind. The new neighbours were squatters. The kids were like wild animals. They seemed to have no boundaries and were out screaming in the corridors until late at night. The mother and father were fond of all night parties, and allowed their off spring to roam in the communal area of the flats while they got boozed up with their equally vile friends. The music and disruption was driving all the neighbours mad. Graffiti had appeared on the communal walls and the once clean and tidy little block now looked neglected and unkempt. So far, nothing had been done about it, despite all the neighbours banding together and bombarding the council with protests. Jay wanted to go next door and shove their bloody sound system where the sun wouldn't shine. Suzy had complained endlessly to the council and her nerves were becoming frazzled. Jay was beginning to think that they needed to move away somewhere. He did not need any more hassle on top of everything else. Jay sipped his orange juice. He could not stop fretting about that ruddy phone call. The social worker had mentioned that they had been found at Jaywick Sands. Martin had held them in a rundown chalet on a holiday campsite. Jay put down his orange juice and stood up suddenly. That was it! Why had it taken him so long for the penny to drop? He ran to the phone and called the victim support officer. Mark Goddard was the police officer who had been assigned to his case after the attack. He had said if Jay remembered anything regarding the attack, he could call him at any time.

"Hello, is that officer Goddard? Look, I'm sorry to call you at the weekend. It's Jay Oakland here. I think I've remembered something important." Mark Goddard was quick to reassure Jay.

"I think I knew Martin Crayford when I was a kid. He had a different name then, that's why I never made the connection before now. When I was about eight, a family called the Renwicks fostered me. They had a child of their own, a year or so older than me called Martin. I 'm sure He resented me, hated having to share his parents attention. I think Martin Crayford was their son. He was a right horrible little bugger even then. I was scared of him, he just behaved very oddly. I didn't stay with them for very long. Anyway, the thing is, they used to take us both to their holiday chalet near Jaywick Sands. A place called Sunnyvale holiday camp. That's where they found Dennis and his mum so I've been told. I'm sure it's not a coincidence. They also had a lock up garage close by. It was in Sunnyvale Road. I remembered it because it always made me laugh. Every time we went there, it rained. I said they should re name it Rainy vale. It was one of the few times I can remember laughing when I was around Martin. It might be worth a look. If they still have the chalet, I bet they kept the lock up too. Martin used to use that garage as a den. He boasted it had electric power in there and a bed chair. He even had a little primus stove. He would never let me go in there, he always told me he kept all his secret stuff there, stuff I would never get to see. If he still has it, it would make a perfect hiding place. I think the police should at least check it out. It might hold some clues."

"Dad, I really need to talk to you, I don't know who else I can turn to. Oh God, Dad, it's such a bloody mess!" Jonny raked his fingers through his hair. He was pacing backwards and forwards across Victor's living room. Victor beckoned his son to come and sit down. Jonny stopped pacing. He did not want to look at his father, he felt too ashamed. He walked over to the fireplace. The photograph of his mother still had pride of place on the mantelpiece and he stared at her beautiful smiling face. "Come and sit down!" Victor said firmly, "I am not holding a conversation with your back!"
Jonny turned then, and sat down. "Sorry Dad. I just don't know where to begin. It's a nightmare. I don't know how I have managed to get myself into such a mess." He raked his fingers through his hair again. He looked distraught and Victor was worried now. He put his hand on his sons arm to reassure him. "Come on, Jon, it's me you're talking to. Just spit it out. You know if I can help in any way I will. It's not Sarah is it? Is there something wrong with the baby?" Jonny saw sudden panic cross his father's face. He shook his head.

119

"Oh no, don't worry, everything is fine with the baby. Sarah is okay. Well, she is now. I don't know how she's going to take the bombshell that's about to drop though." He took a deep breath and then said, "I had another visit from Louise."

Victor sat in grim silence as Jonny told him everything. When Jonny finally ran out of steam, Victor spoke.

"There is no point in me shouting and telling you what an utter bloody fool you've been, Jon. I can tell by your face that you already know that. Now look, if you were as drunk as you say you were that night, there is no way on this earth that you could have done anything with that vile young woman, even if you wanted to. As for fathering a child with her, I doubt she is even pregnant. I think she is just playing games. You said you told her to leave you alone, that you and Sarah were expecting another child together?" Jonny nodded sadly.

"Well, I think she said she was pregnant out of pure spite. She just wants to cause trouble. We shall see about that. I think it's time I had a chat with her father."

"Dad, you can't! Poor Gregg hasn't even buried his wife yet. He must be in a terrible state. He adored Marissa. Imagine how he would feel if he knew about this." Victor considered.

"Well, okay, it's up to you, Jon, but he will have to find out sooner or later, and if I was in his shoes I'd want to know, grieving or not, and for God's sake, don't let Sarah find out from someone else. I wouldn't put it past Louise to go and tell her herself."

Rupert Bingly Warrington had driven from Shropshire to be with his wife. He had been devastated that he did not get there earlier. He had driven down as soon as he got the phone call telling him that his mother in law had passed away. He was puzzled and a little hurt that Louise had not telephoned him sooner. If he had known that Marissa's time was drawing near, he would have dropped everything and come at once. He could not help feeling somewhat excluded. Still, it was too late now. Perhaps Louise had fooled herself into believing her mother would make a remarkable recovery. He could not wait to hold her and offer her some comfort. The funeral was bound to be an ordeal, and he wanted to be by her side to offer as much support as he could. Louise had been so wrapped up in caring for her mother he had hardly seen her for weeks now. He had driven to London whenever he had a free weekend, but Louise had been distant. She had not said much even when he called her each evening to see how she was. He had thought she might have drawn closer to him in the time of crisis but she had pushed him away more often than not. He had been very patient. He knew that grief and stress affected people in different ways. They had only made love once or twice on his numerous visits. He had not wanted to push her, she had enough on her plate, but he had missed her dreadfully.

He pulled into her parents drive and scrunched across the gravel to the big oak front door.

Louise's father had opened the door. Louise was cooking supper in the kitchen. She barely looked at him when he went in to see her. He tried to hide his disappointment and held his arms open to her. Reluctantly she put down the wooden spatula she was holding and went to him. She felt stiff in his arms, but he kissed her cheek and smoothed her hair. "How are you bearing up darling?" he said tenderly, as she pulled away from him. She avoided his eyes but said brightly,

"I'm fine. I'm trying hard for Dad's sake. Supper is nearly ready. Why don't you go and freshen up? You must be tired after your long journey. I'll give you a shout when I'm going to dish up."

It was when they got back from the funeral service that he had found it. The house was full of mourners who had come back to the house to pay their respects. Louise had been remarkably composed during the service; she was still keeping Rupert at arm's length. She looked on autopilot, and Rupert was worried that the shock and grief would inevitably burst out at some point. It all felt very odd. She was downstairs now playing the perfect hostess. She was chatting to a friend of her father when Rupert had come upstairs. The friend's name was Victor Mason. Louise had introduced him and then turned her back on Rupert. He had heard her asking him how his son Jonny was. The man, Victor had looked almost murderous at Louise's enquiry. It had puzzled Rupert, but he had not asked any questions. Gregg had come up to him at that moment and quietly asked him if he would collect coats and make sure everyone was comfortable.

Rupert had come upstairs to put the coats away. Louise had wordlessly piled coats in Rupert's arms as if he was the hired help. He had said nothing, he had been happy to escape the black clad mourners if he was honest. He did not know most of the people downstairs, and certainly did not want to make polite conversation with them. He had met a few at his wedding to Louise but he had not seen them since. He had been relieved to make a justified escape to the sanctuary of the upstairs landing. He had dumped the pile of coats on the bed in the guest bedroom. Then he had stopped off in the bedroom he shared with Louise to hang up his own jacket. It was hot and stuffy in the house and he was feeling uncomfortable. Louise had left her handbag open on the bed. He hated her untidiness. It drove him mad. He had not even seen her come upstairs; she must have been in a rush to get back down to be beside her father. She would laugh at him and call him a neat freak whenever he told her off about her messiness, but he liked order and could not tolerate tardiness. They had a daily help at home who cleared up after Louise, so he hardly noticed any more how messy she was. Since arriving here at her parent's house however, Rupert could not help noticing that she was her old untidy self. He smiled ruefully. She was scatty and undisciplined but he loved her very much.

He picked up the bag to close it, but it was heavier than it looked and he had accidently spilled half of the contents on to the floor. Cursing, he had stooped to pick everything up and there it was. He felt a knife blade pierce his heart as he stared wide-eyed at the photograph. A photograph of a naked man was peeking out of the inside pocket. The man appeared to be asleep and somewhat dishevelled. Rupert recognised the bed he was sleeping in. He had been in it often enough. It was in Louise's Barbican flat. On the back of the photograph, in Louise's handwriting, it said "My darling Jonny Mason." Mason? The man downstairs was called Mason. Louise had been asking about his son Jonny. He sat on the bed and took deep breaths. He looked at his reflection in the dressing table mirror. His face was ashen. He needed to calm down before going downstairs. No point going in all guns blazing. He could not cause a scene, not today of all days.

Rupert hid the photograph in his briefcase and locked it. He finished tidying up, then decided to leave Louise's bag exactly as he had found it.

He left it open with the contents spilling out on their bed. When he had composed himself, he went back downstairs to rejoin the mourners.

Adam picked up the telephone that was ringing shrilly. "You took your time!" Nina said cheekily. Adam grinned. It was always good to hear Nina's voice. "Well pardon me, but I don't spend all my time hanging by the phone. I do have a life, you know. Well, okay, I don't, but a man has to have some pride" Nina laughed. Adam settled himself down on his battered old sofa for a nice long chat. He had come to really look forward to his conversations with Nina. They had a nice easy friendship. "What can I do for you?" Adam said when he had put his feet up. "I just wondered if you were free next Saturday night. You know I said sometimes I am offered cheap tickets to shows through the hotel? Well, I have two tickets to see Blood Brothers. I have heard it's excellent and if you're not doing anything..." her voice trailed off.
"Yeah, count me in" Adam said enthusiastically. Nina sighed with relief. "Good. We get to go to a nice restaurant to eat afterwards, too."
"Even better. What time shall I pick you up?"

Adam opened the door of Sarah and Suzy's shop and said brightly "Good morning my beauties. I have apple donuts and I am willing to share!" He waved the box tantalisingly in front of him and added "Form an orderly queue, and put the ruddy kettle on. I'm gagging for a cuppa!"
"Someone's in a good mood." Suzy said, looking at Adams happy smiling face. She added with a smirk, "Have you seen our Nina recently?" she was gratified to see him blush ever so slightly. Nina had only recently come clean about her and Adam's friendship. She hated keeping secrets from her friends and felt she could cope with the inevitable teasing now. Adam recovered quickly and said
"Oi, watch it madam, I can still withdraw my donuts you know" Suzy giggled, and tried to swipe the cake box. Adam teasingly moved it out of her grasp.
"Don't you dare!" Suzy said, trying and failing to reach the cakes. She gave up in the end and plonked herself back on her stool. She sighed theatrically, then grinned and said, "I have been waiting all morning for one of those donuts. Give it ere. Anyway, I've already had a blow by blow account of your night out together. We girlies tell each other

everything you know. Nina said you had a fantastic time. She said you blubbed like a baby at the end of Blood Brothers."

Adam finally put the box of donuts on the counter. Suzy opened it and licked her lips greedily. "Blimey, is nothing sacred?" He mumbled, grinning. "Anyway, I did not blub..much. I had a piece of dirt in my eye" Suzy rubbed her hands together when she saw the delicious looking plump sugary donuts. She smiled gleefully and said, " Ooow, come to mama." She took out a donut and bit into it. Her face was a picture of rapture. "It's okay anyway. I like a man who's not afraid to show his feminine side."

Adam grinned again. He picked up a donut too and took a big bite. A chunk of apple almost escaped down his chin but he managed to catch it and pop it back into his mouth just as Sarah appeared carrying a tray laden with mugs. "I hope you've saved one of those for me you greedy blighters." she said plonking the tray down beside the donut box. "I'm pigging out for two now you know" She rubbed her tummy and winked wickedly, grabbing the last cake. Her pregnancy did not show much yet but she was still proud to show it off. Adam marvelled that he did not even feel a twinge of emotion about Sarah's bump. He was pleased for her and Jonny, and he wished them well. Nina had really worked wonders for his Sarah crush, he thought incredulously.

Sarah had just swallowed her first bite and was licking the sugar off her lips when the shop door tinkled open. A tall distinguished man entered. "Can I help you?" Suzy said, pleasantly, reluctantly putting down her donut. Why did customers have to interrupt them at cake time? She licked her lips to remove the last remnants of sugar.

"I'm looking for Mrs Mason. Mrs Sarah Mason. I was told she works here?"

"I'm Mrs Mason. How can I help?" Sarah said, putting her own donut down on the counter. She wiped the sugar off her hands hastily.

"I wonder if I could have a private word with you. My name is Rupert Bingly Warrington. I believe you know my wife, Louise."

Sarah could not stop crying. Suzy and Adam did their best to try to calm her, but Sarah could not control the tears once Rupert had finally left the shop. She sat on the stool behind the counter with her hands shredding a tissue. Adam had locked the door and put the closed sign on. He had made fresh mugs of tea for the three of them. Their tea had grown cold while Sarah had had a conversation with Rupert. Their donuts had been forgotten. Suzy and Adam could not help overhearing everything that had been said, even when Sarah had ushered Rupert to the tiny back room for a bit of privacy. By then it was all too late anyway. Suzy and Adam had already heard enough.

Rupert had asked if he could take Sarah somewhere quiet, but Sarah had said whatever it was he had to say he could say it here. She had regretted it almost immediately when he had taken the photograph out of his wallet and waved it for all of them to see. Sarah had gasped in shock. "Where...where did you get this from?" she had managed to say eventually. Her hands had automatically gone protectively to her barely visible baby bump. Rupert regretted not being more discrete. He had not wanted to cause this poor young woman any unnecessary pain. Trying to make amends, he pocketed the photograph hastily and replied quietly "I found it in my wife's handbag on the day of her mother's funeral. I believe your father in law was at the funeral. I'm sorry, I can see you have had an awful shock. I had to do a bit of detective work to find you. I just wondered if you were as much in the dark as I was. It appears that our spouses have been having an affair. I thought you should know."

"There could be a perfectly innocent explanation." Adam had said quickly, trying to help. He shut up when all eyes turned toward him. "I don't see how." Sarah whispered. Her voice was hoarse and she was obviously close to tears. Adam longed to reach out and hold her close. He was suddenly feeling all protective towards her again. Not to mention totally confused. Instead, he said. "Look, don't do anything hasty. At least see what they have to say for themselves." He turned to Rupert. He looked a decent bloke, although he was obviously not seeing him at his best right now. "I know it must be hard, but you can see how upset Sarah is. Why don't you leave her now and let her compose herself a bit? Leave us your contact details and let Sarah get back to you after talking to her husband? Have you asked your wife about this?"

"I can speak for myself you know" Sarah piped up. "Look Mr ..Warrington"

"Please, call me Rupert"

"Look Rupert, I don't know what to say to you really. I know Louise has always had a thing about Jonny. She was obsessed, actually. She once sent him naked photos of herself. I don't know how she got this picture, but you can rest assured I will bloody find out."

"It seems my wife has quite a talent for photography." Rupert said sarcastically. "The photograph was taken in my wife's flat in the Barbican. I recognised it at once. Unless you can think of any other reason why your husband would be naked in her bed, I'd say the evidence is pretty compelling. Yes, I have spoken to her of course. I confronted her. I caught her searching her bag frantically for the photo. She didn't even try to deny it. She says they are in love. She said your husband gave her two little teddy bears, antique teddy bears as a present. Love tokens, she called them. He opened the briefcase he was carrying. He took out the two Schuco bears. Sarah gasped in shock. She remembered when Jonny had bought those bears. He had bid for them at an auction. Rupert snapped his briefcase closed with the bears locked inside. "I can see you recognise them. You might be interested to know that my wife and I are no longer together. She has left me and I don't have a clue where she is."

Adam had taken Sarah to his flat in Granville Square. She was too upset to go home. He was worried what she might do to Jonny in this state anyway. She had threatened to cut his balls off while she was at the shop. He had got a vivid picture of Nina with her cheese wire in his head at that remark. They had left Suzy clearing up the remains of their discarded apple donuts. "Don't worry hun, I'll pick up the girls. You go and sort yourself out and call me later," Suzy had said soothingly as Adam ushered Sarah out of the door.

Sarah sat on Adam's sofa and he handed her a mug of tea. She took it and sipped the hot liquid gratefully. "Thanks" she said, trying to smile. Then her face crumpled again. "Oh, I'm sorry, Adam. You don't need all my troubles." Adam sat down next to her and put his arm around her. He gave her shoulder a little squeeze. "Heh, don't worry, what are friends for?"

He was such a decent bloke Sarah could not bear it. She could not help it. A huge sob escaped her lips. "What the hell am I going to do?"

126

Nina had tried not to mind about Sarah staying at Adam's flat. Sarah had been at Adam's for over a month now. There was no reason to be jealous, after all. Adam and she were just mates. They got on like the proverbial house on fire, but there was no romantic spark. She had no cause to be jealous. Even though she felt that if Adam was not such a decent bloke he would jump on Sarah's bones given the first bit of encouragement. It should not have mattered. She knew too that Sarah would never look at any one else other than her Jon. Even a blind man could see that. She was also certain Sarah would never do anything with Adam because she knew that Nina and he were friends. No, Sarah would soon get over this present hiccup, Nina was certain. It had all been really upsetting. Jonny had begged and pleaded with Sarah, telling her that she could not take his daughter away from him. Poor Adam had intervened and tried to assure Jon that nothing was going on between him and Sarah. Nina did not know if Jon believed him, but he had accepted the situation in the end. He had no choice. He had told Sarah that he had got drunk on the night he had stormed out and had gone to a wine bar. Louise had been there. He had hoped by telling Sarah the truth at last it would make things better, but Sarah had been furious. She had said she was leaving. She had no idea at the time where she was going. She had not wanted her mother to be stressed about their marital problems. That was why she had taken up Adam's offer of a roof over her head. Things had now settled down into a routine, of sorts. Nina had still gone round regularly and Sarah and Adam had always been pleased to see her. Why was it then that Nina was so worked up? She dipped another chocolate Hobnob in her tea and put her feet up. She put the telly on. It was a documentary about poaching in Africa so she quickly switched over. She could not bear seeing animals slaughtered for greed. It was too upsetting. She switched on a quiz show instead. That was more like it. A bit of mindless rubbish was all she could cope with at the moment. She turned down the volume as the clapping and forced laughter boomed out at her.
The phone rang, interrupting her thoughts. She picked up the receiver. It was Adam. Talk of the devil, she told herself, grinning. She caught sight of her reflection in her mirror that hung on the wall above her fireplace. Her face had lit up at the sound of Adam's voice.

Reality suddenly dawned on her. How thoroughly she had deceived herself she thought with a jolt. Bugger it, she told herself sitting down with a thump. She had fallen for Adam without even realising it.

Suzy lay in bed next to Jay. She relished the warmth of him, and listened to his heart beating. She had missed this closeness so much when he had been in hospital. She felt so sorry for Sarah and for Jonny too, they must be missing this special closeness. She could not resist, and sat up a little to kiss Jay's lips. "I didn't know you were still awake." He said softly. "You okay, Suze?" Suzy shook her head, and then realised Jay could not see in the dark, so she sighed and said, "Not really. I can't help worrying about Sarah and Jonny. Sarah is so unhappy. I wish there was something I could do. Maybe if.."
"Don't interfere." Jay interrupted. Suzy protested, but Jay was insistent. "Listen Suze, I know it's hard, but they have to sort this out for themselves. They won't thank you for meddling."
Suzy sighed again. "I know you're right, but it's so bloody hard. I do wish sometimes I had a magic wand. Poor Sarah badly needs a Fairy Godmother right now."

CHAPTER TEN

Joycie had let herself into Suzy's flat with her spare key to pick up Amy's raincoat and little umbrella. It was clouding over, and Joycie thought she had better be safe than sorry. She was with Carrie. They had had a nice afternoon drinking tea together in Carrie's flat. They were going to collect the girls from school now. Suzy and Sarah were at work in the shop, but they were both going to do some food shopping after work. Joycie and Carrie enjoyed helping out. Carrie was looking very well these days. She was singing to Bobby Jay in his pushchair while Joycie popped into Suzy's hallway to pick up the umbrella and find Amy's raincoat. The communal area of Harold Laskie House smelled of fresh paint. The council had finally got their act together, Joycie thought. The squatters had been evicted at last and poor old Narky Norris had been able to come home to his flat again. All traces of the graffiti and squatters had been erased. It was such a relief for everyone. Joycie said she wouldn't be a minute so Carrie waited and entertained little Bobby Jay. They would pick up the girls, give them a bite to eat and Suzy and Sarah would send Jay and Jonny to collect the kids once they had got home from work.

Joycie rang Carrie every day to check on her, and they met several times a week. Joycie wondered when Sarah was going to tell her mother that she had separated from Jonny. She had been so shocked when Suzy had told her. They had always seemed so happy. Poor Sarah was in bits, but did not want her mum to know yet, in case the worry made her ill again. Sarah was staying with Adam the market inspector. It all seemed very complicated to Joycie, but she knew better than to interfere and had promised not to say anything to Carrie. It was proving to be very awkward, however. Carrie was nobody's fool, and she knew something was not right. Joycie did not know how much longer she could keep up the pretence of not knowing.

As Joycie closed Suzy's front door and locked it, Carrie said, "Did you hear that noise, Joyce? I think it was coming from old Narky's flat next door?" Joycie shrugged and shook her head but then they both heard a loud bump. Joycie knocked on Suzy's neighbour's door. " Mr Norris? Are you in there?" there was no reply. Joycie knocked again. There was only silence. "You don't think those bloody squatters have come back do you?" she said to Carrie. "Better have a look to find out" Carrie said in a worried voice. Joycie looked through the letterbox. "Oh my Christ, He's on the floor. I think he's dead!"

Linda Patterson was tired. It had been a busy and noisy afternoon covering for this class of six year olds. Being a supply teacher was a lot harder than getting to know a class of your own. She did not know the children in this class and trying to remember who collected them at home time was a nightmare. She had been left instructions from the head teacher about the two little girls called Amy Oakland and Lydia Mason. The two girls were best friends. Their grandmothers picked them up on Fridays. Amy was a dear little girl with long dark hair. She had gone off happily enough. She had been the first child to go home as the caretaker opened the gates. The class had all lined up eventually and had been waiting in the playground. The rain had not started yet, although the dark grey clouds overhead told her that the rain was imminent. Amy's friend Sarah had gone back inside to collect her umbrella. She had left it on her coat peg. Linda had been busy watching the sweet little red haired girl inside and had turned just as Amy skipped out of the gates holding onto her grandmother's hand. It had been quite a job to get all the other children to behave. The children always played up supply teachers. They sensed any hesitance or lack of confidence and would push and test the capabilities of the newcomer to the limit. It was never easy and this had been Linda Patterson's first day at Moreland Primary school. She had had a nightmare in the morning with the juniors and now she had been thrown in at the deep end with this class of infants. The infant class teacher, Miss Cotton had been on playground duty that morning when a football kicked by one of the juniors had hit her full in the face and knocked out her two front teeth. Linda had stepped into the breach to take over so that Claire Cotton could go off and get her teeth fixed urgently. The juniors had temporarily joined another class. Linda wondered how the junior teacher was coping with sixty children. The school nurse had put Claire Cotton in a taxi with her two front teeth floating in a jar filled with milk. Hopefully the dentist would be able to work a bit of magic and allow her to smile again. It had certainly been a frenetic day, but it was nearly over.

There was only one more child waiting to be collected. Two women rushed into the playground obviously frantic at being late. One was pushing a little boy in a pushchair who was giggling loudly under his rain cover, obviously loving being pushed very fast. Linda Patterson smiled expectantly while the women got their breath back. "That's my Nana" said Lydia Mason, the little red haired girl, pointing towards Carrie. She let go of Miss Patterson's hand and skipped towards Carrie's outstretched arms. "Oh sweetheart, I'm sorry for being late." Carrie said, bending down to give Lydia a big kiss and a hug. "Poor old Mr Norris had a nasty fall again. Nanny and auntie Joycie had to call an ambulance to come and help him."

"Oh, poor Mr Norris. Is he better now?" Lydia said, hugging Carrie.

"Yes, don't worry. That nice lady from upstairs, Julie Harrison, came down to wait for the ambulance. We heard it coming as we came to get you and Amy. We rushed all the way but you know poor nanny, I can't run too fast." Lydia smiled and kissed her gran. "That's all right, Nan. You run quick for an old lady" she said, trying to be diplomatic. Carrie laughed out loud, but stopped when she heard Joycie's concerned voice.

"Excuse me, but where is Amy?" A worried Joycie asked the teacher who was just going back into the classroom. Linda Patterson turned, and looked a bit perplexed.

"She went home with her grandmother." she said curtly as if talking to a recalcitrant child. Joycie felt herself bristle immediately at this young girls patronising tone. She wondered where Amy's regular class teacher was. It wasn't like Miss Cotton to be off sick. "But I'm her grandmother" she said, forcefully, panic now rising in her throat. "Who are you, anyway? Where's Miss Cotton?"

Linda Patterson tried to remain calm. It was not easy as the woman in front of her was shouting now. "I am Miss Paterson, the supply teacher. Miss Cotton had an emergency dental appointment today. I was left instructions that Amy would be picked up from school by her grandmother. I thought.." Her voice trailed away as Joycie began shouting again. She felt her heart begin to pound. She did her best to calm the poor woman down. It was impossible however. It appeared that the child, this woman's granddaughter Amy Oakland had been abducted.

131

As soon as Jay walked into the room, Suzy flung herself into his arms and sobbed on his shoulder. Jay tried in vain to soothe her. "Oh Jay, not our baby, not our darling girl. I can't lose another baby. I can't bear it. Where is she, Jay?" she beat frantically on his chest, as if he would magically produce their beloved daughter from inside his jacket.

Jay was too emotional to reassure his distraught wife. He hugged her and kissed her but no words came. Amy had been missing for two hours now. He had driven home like a lunatic as soon as he had been informed about his daughter's disappearance. He sat now with Suzy by his side, feeling utterly helpless. He had taken Bobby Jay from Joycie who had been trying to soothe him. The child was fretful and had noticed the tension in the room. Jay cuddled his son close and drank in the smell of his soft skin.

Two police officers were in his living room, along with a pale and tearful Joycie, and Suzy's dad, Bob. Suzy's brother Robert came in carrying a tea tray.

One of the police officers tried to pacify Suzy who had stood up and paced the floor. Another officer had put Suzy's food shopping away. Suzy had opened her front door and rushed to answer the telephone when she had finally got in after work. She had dropped her shopping bags on the hall floor and left them there in her panic at hearing the news that Amy was missing. Her frantic mum had been trying in vain to contact her. She had left work in high spirits and had done her food shop after work. Sarah had told her she was going to see Jonny. They had had a visitor at the shop earlier. Louise had shown up. It had all seemed unreal. Just when she had thought things were getting better. She had hummed happily all the way round Sainsbury's. All the time she had been rooting around the freezer cabinets, her precious baby was missing. She felt sick. She should have picked her up from school herself.

The rain was now beating at the windowpanes demanding attention. She shook off the officer's arm angrily. "We should be out there on the streets looking for her." She looked over at her brother. "I don't want any more bloody tea!" Rob did not mind his sister's angry words. His heart was breaking for her. The police had told them to stay at home but it was tortuous. They had told the police as much as they could.

132

"Look, I don't know about you, but I'd feel a lot happier if we were out there. At least we would be doing something constructive." Rob said, putting the unwanted tea tray down on the coffee table. "Do you really think that bastard Martin what's his name might have her?" he whispered to Jay as Suzy left the room to go to the toilet again. Her bladder always let her down when she was too stressed. Jay stood up. He kissed Bobby Jays head and put him down on the floor. "I don't know Rob. I don't know anything anymore. You're right though, we should be out there. I can't stand it anymore. Let's go."

"I'm coming too" said Suzy's dad, Bob. He pulled on his jacket that was resting on the arm of Suzy's sofa. The police officer opened her mouth to speak but Bob Pond held his hand up furiously. "Don't try to stop us love," he told her, "If that bastard Martin has got our little girl, we'll find him. We've wasted enough time as it is." Suzy came back into the room. Bobby Jay toddled over to her and hugged her legs. She bent down automatically and stroked his silky hair. Then she stood up and blinked back fresh tears.

"I don't think Martin Crayford has taken her." She said quietly. All eyes turned towards her. "The teacher said a woman took her." She added. "That doesn't mean anything!" Jay said, annoyed at the delay. He wanted to go and search the streets and find his baby. "He could have sent his mother." He looked at the police officer accusingly and hissed, "Did any one bother to check out the garages near that holiday camp? I told the police about that ages ago! He could have been locked up again by now if they'd checked them out! I bet he has been there, it might have had some clues."

Suzy shook her head. "No Jay, think about it. I don't think that Martin has anything to do with it. Amy is a good girl; she wouldn't go with a stranger. She's sensible for her age, you know she is. She knew whoever took her. That teacher said she heard Amy call her nanny." A look of realisation washed over her face, and she said excitedly "Oh god Jay, I think it was Violet who took her!"

Louise had fled the house after the terrible row with Rupert. She had never seen him so angry or hurt before. He had stood with her father and they had both looked appalled. Rupert had found the photograph of Jonny. She felt like one of Rupert's accused clients in a courtroom, as he waved it angrily in front of her, demanding an explanation. She sat in stony silence on her parent's sofa and squirmed as he threw accusations at her. Her father just stood silently behind Rupert. It was his look of disapproval that she found so hard to bear. She felt sick. She had always been able to wrap her father around her little finger. He had always spoiled her and given her anything she had ever asked for. It was ironic really. The only thing he could not give her was Jonny Mason. She had tried to argue, but it had been futile. Anything she said just seemed to make Rupert even angrier, so she had just sat there, listening to him ranting. She knew she had been stupid. She deserved all she got, she realised that now. Everything he was saying about her was true. He had called her a fantasist and an ungrateful spoiled brat. She had not meant for things to go this far. It had all spiralled out of control. She had wanted to play it cool this time. She thought she had made all her juvenile mistakes years ago as far as Jonny was concerned, anyway. She really had not meant her harmless little fantasy to reach this stage. If only she could take back the stupid words she had said to Jonny. She had just been so jealous. She had not been able to stop herself. After all her efforts to try to gain his affections, he was still totally in love with that wretched woman Sarah. Then he had to go and get her pregnant again. The thought of her darling Jonny playing happy families with another woman was too much to bear. She tried not to picture Jon lying with his wife, making love to her. It hurt her so much she could not stand it. She could not get the image out of her head though. She had not intended to tell him she too was pregnant, but once the words had flown from her lips, it was too late. They had tumbled out of her mouth, like a hapless magician whose card trick had gone horribly wrong. The words had spilled out all over the place. She could not erase Jonny's look of absolute horror from her mind. She had felt she had to keep up the pretence. She had readily lit up a whole box of fireworks. It was a very dangerous game, and now her deception had exploded in her face. She felt panic rising as Rupert finally ran out of abuse to hurl at her. He had said he wanted a divorce. Good grief, she had been a naïve fool. She realised that she cared for Rupert a great deal, and she did not want to go through a divorce.

It was her father's turn now. Rupert had sat on the sofa opposite and had his head in his hands. Louise had not meant to hurt him like this.

She felt so terribly guilty. She had not realised the depths of Rupert's feelings for her. Fresh guilt washed over her as she saw how much she had hurt her already devastated father too. She had ruined everything. She wanted to go and try to comfort her husband, say something to make things right between them, but her father's eyes had her pinned to her seat. She looked up tearfully at her father. She had always been a daddy's girl. He had spoilt her for as long as she could remember. He had always made excuses for her brattish behaviour, had made light of it in the past and even defended her to her mother. Now she knew she had pushed him too far. His look of disgust made her quiver.

"My god, look at you!" he fumed. "You have no idea of how many lives you have ruined, have you? I'm just grateful that your poor mother is not here to witness this latest debacle." Louise felt a tear roll down her cheek at this. She had been such a disappointment to her parents.

"Don't give me any of your waterworks either!" her father continued, "You have to stop this stupid, selfish behaviour Louise. Now tell me, and I want the truth or God help you, did you sleep with Jonny Mason or is this whole bloody nightmare just another figment of your imagination? Because I tell you now this is the last straw. I thought you had grown up a bit, got over your obsession. What has Jon Mason got to offer you that you haven't already got with your husband? Hmm? Acting like a stupid little fool when you were a teenager was bad enough but..."

"Stop it!" Louise screamed, "Just stop it! I can't stand it anymore!" she felt cornered, like a wounded animal. She had to get herself out of this mess. Even now, she could not face reality. "I am sorry I've caused so much trouble, truly I am, but we are in love. I am sorry to hurt you, Rupert, but I love Jonny Mason. I always have. I should never have married you. I know Jonny loves me too...deep down. He doesn't love his wife, he loves me!"

"Enough of your bloody lies!" her father said, looking like he was about to explode. "I have confronted poor Jonny all ready, and he says he has not got a clue what happened. He went out one night, and he got blind drunk. You popped up like the malevolent little Jack in the box you are. He woke up in your bed with no idea how he got there. I believe him. I know only too well what a scheming, conniving little bitch you are! All he wants is to salvage his marriage! He loves his wife with all his heart

and he rues the day he ever clapped eyes on you. I can't say I blame
him, either. You are an embarrassment, Louise."
" No! No! it's not true!" Louise was crying in earnest now. Her father
sighed with impatience.
"Grow up you stupid woman! Face reality for once in your bloody life!
Jonny can't stand the sight of you, the poor man! The sooner you admit
it, the better!"
"Dad, please...I..I'm sorry. Okay, I ..may have exaggerated slightly...."
She laughed nervously, hoping it would lighten the situation. She
misread things as usual. It was then that her father slapped her. It was
one single stinging blow. Louise gasped in shock and looked at her
father, holding her hand over her stinging cheek. She glanced at Rupert.
Her husband's disgusted face mirrored her fathers.
She pushed past her father and fled. They did not try to stop her.

She had gone to the Barbican flat. She knew it would be the first place
that her father and Rupert would look if they wanted to find her, but
she had to escape. They had left her in peace for three days.
 She had tried in vain to speak to Jonny. She had rung the shop but he
had hung up when he heard her voice. She had not given up and rang
him continuously throughout the day. Eventually he had said wearily
"Louise, don't ever ring or try to contact me again. You have successfully
managed to ruin my life and cause untold hurt to my family. I don't
know what goes on in that warped little head of yours, but just piss off
and leave me alone. I'm done being polite to you. The truth is I can't
stand you, I never could. I hope I never see you again for as long as I
live."
In tears, she had rung Camilla. She poured out her heart to her, not
thinking for a second that Camilla would be anything less than
supportive. "Can you come round?" Louise had sniffled, "I really need
you."
 Camilla had turned up an hour later, with a bottle of Chablis. Louise had
begun to whine about how hard done by she was the minute the wine
had been uncorked. Camilla sat for a while with her wine glass in hand
not saying anything. Eventually Louise had stopped talking, expecting
Camilla to make soothing and sympathetic noises in response to her out
pouring of self-pity. However, Camilla had taken her completely by

surprise. "I don't know how you live with yourself," she had said coldly. Louise had opened her mouth to protest, but Camilla had silenced her with a look of utter icy disapproval. "Louise, when are you going to wake up to yourself? Have you any idea what a selfish, juvenile, spoiled brat you really are? I'm sorry, Lou, but you need to be told. Wake up! That poor Jonny Mason! He has told you repeatedly that he isn't interested in you. You're like some kind of demented stalker. What about his poor wife? You know you've split them up, don't you? What if they end up getting a divorce? What then? Do you think you can sweep in and ride off into the Technicolor sun set with Jonny? It's never going to happen. All these years I've had to listen to you wittering on about him. You have a husband who adores you, yet still it's Jonny you go on about. You can't have him, and that's why you want him. I don't think you even really care about him, it's just driven you mad that you never got a chance. Why do you feel you can ruin people's lives? What are you going to do if poor Rupert divorces you? It's horrible getting divorced, Lou. I know, I've been through it. It nearly destroyed me, but when I needed you, you were not there. You always changed the subject, as usual. Every time I rang you, hoping for a few words of comfort I couldn't get a word in because you were raving again about Jonny and how heartbroken you were because you couldn't have him! I need you now, Lou. I wanted to talk to you that night in the wine bar, but all you cared about was Jonny. You didn't even ask me why I was late, did you? Well, I had been to see my doctor. I had an abnormal smear test. I found out yesterday that I have cervical cancer and I'm bloody terrified. I don't want to go through this on my own, but you're too wrapped up in your own selfish world to help me!"

Louise put down her wine glass and realised what a complete idiot she had been. Camilla was very red in the face after her outburst, and Louise could only sit in stunned silence. She had been outraged when Camilla had begun; she had not wanted to hear it. However, she slowly realised with utter shame that Camilla was telling the truth. She was spoilt, and self-centred, and had been a terrible friend. How had she managed to convince herself that she had any chance with Jonny? It was all just daydreams. She only wanted him because she knew she could not have him, Camilla was right. She had once wanted a rocking horse as a child. An old fashioned dapple-grey one, with a beautiful polished wooden stand and a silvery grey mane and tail. She had seen it in Harrods. Her mother and father had taken her there as a treat. The wooden rocking horse had cost a fortune and her mother had said they could not afford it, and it would take up too much room. Louise had begged and pleaded, had a tantrum in the middle of the busy toy department. It was one of the only times Louise ever remembered her parents refusing her anything. She could still remember the tutting and disapproving looks from other shoppers as her mortified mother had dragged her from the store. She had not given up, however. She had become obsessed. She had cried, begged and pleaded every day for months. She had tantrum after tantrum once they had gone home and still her mother had refused to give in. Louise had tried every trick in the book to persuade her mother. She had promised never to ask for anything else ever. She had sworn to be good, to work hard at school, to do all her chores. Then her birthday had arrived and her father took her out to his work van. He had a large green van that he used for collecting antiques for his shop in Hampstead. He had given her the keys and told her to unlock the back of the van. Inside had been the rocking horse. Louise had cried with excitement and had flung her arms around her father with delight. She had smirked at her mother, who had been furious with her father for giving in.

However, her joy at her victory had been short lived. She had grown bored with the rocking horse very quickly, and the dapple grey horse had stood unloved and gathering dust in her room ever since. It was still there, in her old bedroom in her parents' house. It stood as a testament to her spoilt demands. She flushed at the memory. She wondered if she would have grown bored with Jonny, if she had ever had the chance. She had never considered that possibility. Her fantasy had never, in all the years she had hankered after him, gone into the realities of sustaining a relationship. She had day dreamed about making love, sweet-talking under the sheets, laughing and joking together. It had never occurred to her that mundane reality would soon bring her back to earth with a bump. She was horrified with herself. She thought of Jonny's pregnant wife Sarah. Of Jonny, all alone, separated from the woman he loved. They even had a little girl. She must be missing her daddy. Jonny's face had always lit up when he mentioned her. He obviously adored her. She looked at Camilla. She had never been there for her, and yet Camilla had always come running whenever she clicked her spoilt fingers. She vowed to be there from now on, to support her and see her through her ordeal.

A huge tear rolled down Louise's cheek. Camilla put her arms around her and Louise sobbed.

Louise knew she had to try to make amends. She had lost everything and it slowly dawned on her just what she had let slip through her fingers. She could not get the hurt look she had seen in Rupert's eyes out of her mind. She had not realised how much he cared for her. His face had been devastated. She had been so wrapped up in her own selfish little fantasy world that she had trampled everyone in her path. How utterly selfish she had been. Well, it was time to grow up and face it all head on, she told herself decisively. It would take all her courage but she knew what she had to do.

Sarah could not believe her eyes when Louise walked into the shop. She did not have her usual cocky smirking expression on her face, either. She actually looked quite penitent. Sarah still had the urge to kill her though. Before she could say anything however, Suzy stopped dusting the display of cards and growled, "Look what the cat dragged in! What the fucking hell do you want? Haven't you caused enough trouble?"

Louise looked at Suzy shamefacedly, and then turned to face Sarah. Her own face looked genuinely distraught. Sarah felt almost sorry for her.

"I.. I wondered if I could speak to you Sarah? I haven't come to cause any trouble, I promise. I have come to apologise and tell you the truth." Sarah and Suzy exchanged astonished glances. They had never seen Louise behave decently before. Sarah wondered briefly if she had been abducted by aliens and been cloned with a nicer more amenable double. She could not help but be wary. Suzy spoke first. "Shall I put the kettle on?" she said, without taking her eyes off Louise. She held the duster in her hands as if she wanted to throttle Louise with it. Suzy eyed her with suspicion, as if she was an unexploded bomb that could detonate at any moment. Sarah replied, "Yes please."

She too could not look away from Louise. Suzy went off to make tea. She called over her shoulder sarcastically to Louise "One lump of arsenic or two?"

Louise licked her lips nervously then she said in a low voice to Sarah "Look, I lied. I'm sorry, so sorry. I am a stupid, spoilt, selfish brat. I know that now. Jonny never touched me. I made the whole thing up. The only crime Jonny committed was to get falling down drunk. Even that wasn't really his fault, it was mine. He tried to refuse the drinks I kept buying him, but I insisted. He nearly passed out on the pavement outside the wine bar. He wanted to get away from me, but I followed him out. All he wanted was to come home to you and make it up. I could tell you must have had an argument. He didn't tell me anything, he's far too loyal to you... I bundled him into a black cab and took him to my flat. I undressed him, put him to bed, and took that wretched photo. I was so wrapped up in my own stupid dream I lost touch with reality." She paused for breathe. Suzy was back with mugs of tea. She placed them on the counter. She pondered over whether to leave them to it and make herself scarce, but was too nosy to actually leave. Instead, she stood beside Sarah and listened, her lips set firmly in a straight line as Louise carried on.

Sarah was sitting behind the counter. Her eyes were full of tears but she remained silent. Louise took a deep breath and continued. "I was so jealous of you." She looked sorrowfully at Sarah. "I never even thought how you must be feeling. I just saw you as an obstacle in my way. It was no use, though. No matter what horrible tricks I tried, Jonny will never be mine, because he really does love you with all his heart." A tear trickled down her cheek and she let it fall. "Please...please don't let him slip away from you. Otherwise all this..well, it will all be for nothing. He is heartbroken and it's all my fault. Please let me do something good for a change, I want to put my mistakes right if I can. I've ruined so many lives. I have to try to salvage something. My husband will never forgive me for what I did, and I don't blame him. I've lost everything, and I didn't even know just how much I had until It was gone. My father is in pieces. He is so ashamed of me. Please don't let me ruin your lives as well."

It seemed very quiet in the shop after Louise had left. Sarah looked stunned and Suzy eventually said "What are you doing sitting there, you daft mare? Go and see that husband of yours." Sarah grinned and said quietly, "I'll get my coat"

The doorbell had rung. Louise had been sitting crying quietly after the visit to Sarah's shop. She looked at the clock. She had not realised it had been over an hour since she had come home. It had grown dark and she had not even noticed. She stood up listlessly, turned on a lamp and then opened the door. She was not expecting it to be the person she saw in front of her.

They had argued on the doorstep. It had all happened so quickly. She ushered him inside when an irate neighbour poked their head round their own front door and demanded they both keep the noise down.

He wanted her to go and apologise and admit she had been lying all along. She tried telling him that she had already done so, but he did not seem to hear her. He had a vacant expression in his eyes, and it scared her. Oh good grief, what the hell had she done to him?

He had insisted she go with him, grabbing her by the arm and frog marching her out of the flat. He pulled her towards the car park, shoving her roughly into the passenger seat. She had never seen him behave like this before. She decided it would be best to humour him. Maybe if she talked calmly to him, she would be able to penetrate his thoughts and get him to understand. She had done the right thing at last, hadn't she? Sarah had said she would speak to Jonny. Louise had left the little shop feeling so much better. She hoped that in time Jonny and Sarah would be able to forgive her.

It was his silence now that terrified her the most. They drove away from the Barbican, along Upper Street through the evening traffic towards Highbury corner. His hands gripped the steering wheel and his face had a coldness to it that made him almost unrecognisable. They passed the shops along Holloway road and Louise eventually sat in silence, starring out of the passenger window at the blurred images that passed. The rain had steamed up the glass and people were just colours sliding by. He would not speak to her, so she had given up trying. She had tried using a calm voice, tried explaining that it was all okay now. He had not even glanced at her. He stared at the road ahead. The silence was uncomfortable. She avoided looking at him and wiped the steam away from the glass so she had something to focus on. She gripped her handbag and watched the passers-by hurrying home with their umbrellas up. She had only just managed to grab her bag before he had frog marched her out of the flat. The car crawled along through the busy traffic towards Archway and on toward Highgate. She could hear her pounding heart booming in her ears. It seemed to beat a rhythm with the windscreen wipers swishing away the driving rain. It was raining heavily now. The traffic had thinned out and lights were beginning to come on in the street lamps and surrounding houses. She pictured people turning on their televisions and beginning to get supper ready and she longed to escape and go home. She swallowed hard as she realised she did not have a proper home anymore. She had made such a mess of everything.

Finally, he had pulled over in a side street and parked the car. The street was familiar but she could not remember what it was called. She used to play with a little girl who lived in one of the houses along here. She had not been here since she was a child. They were by the woods. It was a quiet road, there was no one about. Not even the usual dog walkers were out in this rain. She had loved playing in the woods as a little girl. In the school holidays, her parents had brought her here for picnics. They used to pick blackberries from the hedgerows here. Her mother would make wonderful blackberry and apple pies when they got home. She wondered what he wanted, why had he not taken her home? The rain drummed on the roof of the car, but he opened the door and came round to the passenger side.

He dragged her from the passenger seat and pulled her across the pavement, in amongst the dense woodland. "Where are you taking me? Can't you just drive me home? I haven't been in these woods for years. It's hardly the night for a pleasant stroll." She tried to keep the fear out of her voice. Her heart was pounding in her ears. "Please, talk to me. I have done my best to put things right, I really have. I went to see Sarah. Oh, please, I can't bear this silence! What …what do you want? Why have you brought me here?"

He ignored her. He did not even look at her. He had locked his hand firmly around her wrist and she had no choice but to follow him along the dark path in amongst the trees.

She smelled the damp wood and felt the icy cold raindrops fall from the leaves onto her hair as he pulled her deeper into the undergrowth. The bushes scratched at her face and legs, and she begged him to slow down. She was crying now, pleading with him to tell her what he wanted, where they were going, but he remained silent. Her handbag was wrenched cruelly from her grasp as it snagged on a bramble but he would not let her stop to retrieve it. The rain began to fall harder and despite the canopy of the trees, she was soaked through. Finally, he stopped at a small clearing and stood over her, panting. She trembled as he towered above her rain splashed face. He forced her back ward until she was leaning against a tall oak. She could hear his laboured breathing, and could almost smell his rage. She could not bear the look on his face. She could just make out his features in the twilight. She felt his hot breath upon her cheek. She could hear traffic in the distance but no one was around on a night like this. She shivered. Her teeth were chattering. Realisation dawned on her. He was going to punish her. He had brought her to a place he knew they would not be interrupted. "Go on then" she whispered, "Get it over with. I know I deserve it."

She looked down at her feet, ready now for what she knew was coming. The first blow was almost a relief. She staggered and let a tiny scream escape from her lips as his hand hit the side of her head. It hurt, but she almost welcomed the pain. She deserved to be punished, she told herself. He would forgive her after this she knew he would. It would all be all right, it would wipe the slate clean. It would soon be over, and then she would go home to her parent's house. It was not far from here. She prepared herself for the next blow. She raised her arms instinctively to defend herself, breathing deeply. She thought he would soon stop.

He was frenzied now, out of control. She staggered as the blows began to rain down on her. This was not what she expected. She screamed at him to leave her alone, and she tried again to tell him how sorry she was.

It was no use. He was beyond reason now, unhinged. Terror seized her as she realised he was not going to stop.

She tried to run but he was too quick. Her high heels had stuck in the muddy ground and he had his hands around her throat in an instant. He pulled her up, tightening his grip around her neck. She could not breathe. He was swearing at her now, calling her names. He told her she was a lying scheming little bitch, that he was ashamed of her, and he had to put a stop to her scheming once and for all. With every word, he squeezed her throat tighter. She kicked, struggled, tried desperately to loosen his hands around her throat. She felt the panic rising, and clawed at him to break free. Her eyes bulged and her tongue hung obscenely from between her lips as frantically she tried to prize his hands away. His face began to swim before her vision.

Soon everything went black and Louise sank down limply on to the wet bark amongst the trees.

Jonny lay on the sofa. He had the television on, but was not paying attention to it. There was a celebrity who he recognised but did not know his name screaming excitedly. He had no idea what he was saying. He had the whole house to himself at the moment. Victor and Marlayna had allowed him a day off and they were at the shop. Victor had rung him a little while ago to let him know they were going out for dinner after closing up. They had asked him if he wanted to join them, but Jonny had said no, he had a book to read, and he had just made something to eat. He could not concentrate on anything though. He put the novel down and had switched the TV on. He had read the same sentence in his book four times and it still had not penetrated. He had only switched the TV on for some background noise. The flat was so quiet without Sarah and Lydia there and he could not bear the silence. He picked at the toasted sandwich he had made without enthusiasm. He was hungry but could not be bothered to cook dinner. He took a bite from the sandwich when the doorbell rang. He put his plate down and got up. Shady looked hopefully at the plate but curiosity got the better of her and she followed Jonny downstairs to the door to see who the caller was.

Jonny was thrilled and delighted to find Sarah on the doorstep. He felt his heart begin to race at the sight of her. Shady threw herself at Sarah, wagging her rudder like tail ecstatically. Jonny wanted to do exactly the same but he tried to contain himself. Bending down to fuss the wagging dog, Sarah said, "Can we talk, Jon? I need to speak to you."

Sarah followed Jonny upstairs. Shady settled herself down next to her, resting an adoring head on Sarah's lap. She wagged her tail happily, as Sarah stroked her velvety ears absentmindedly. She had refused the tea that Jonny had offered her. She was nervous. It felt odd being home again. She had not been inside the flat since she had tearfully packed her things and left. Jonny saw Lydia regularly but he came to Adams house and collected her. It was stilted and unnatural, but they had all tried to be civilised for Lydia's sake. Sarah could still picture a distraught Jonny begging her to stay. She closed her eyes briefly to clear her mind of the heart breaking images.

Jonny sat anxiously on the edge of the armchair waiting to hear what Sarah had to say. She looked over at his concerned face. Her heart ached at his dishevelled appearance. She had never seen him like this before she left. He had always been so cool and well turned out. She took a deep breath.

"I had a visitor at the shop, Jon." Sarah said eventually, still stroking Shady's ears. "It was Louise." She added quietly.

Jonny opened his mouth to speak, but Sarah put up her hand to silence him. "It's okay, she explained everything. She told me what really happened. I've never seen her look..I dunno, humble, I suppose. She told me she had made the whole thing up. I think I knew all along, really. She begged me to try and put things right between us." Sarah looked at Jonny. She longed to reach out and hug him. She could almost touch the pain in his eyes. It mirrored her own. She swallowed hard. A golf ball had risen up in her throat and her voice was thick with emotion. "Jon, I want us to try again.No, please, let me finish" she said, as Jonny had reached out for her. "I..I need you to understand what you did to me. I have never been able to fully explain it. I have tried but it always ended in a row and I couldn't get the words out before. How it felt when I saw that ..that bloody photo. I felt betrayed. You let me down, Jon. You left me to go out and get blind drunk when I needed you most and to make matters worse, you ended up in that woman's bed. Now, I believe that nothing happened, but I can't get over you putting me through all that in the first place. I want to, I really do. Lyddy misses you so much. She cries for you at night, and she cries for Shady." Sarah let out a little sob. "Oh hell, Jon I bloody miss you so much too...I am sorry I kept such a big secret from you about my mum, but I was afraid you would react exactly the way you did when you found out." Jonny came and sat next to her then. Sarah could smell his nearness and it was making it hard to carry on, but she knew if she did not say this now she never would. She took a deep breath and continued.

145

"I don't want to do this baby malarkey thing on my own either." She looked at Jonny's pain wrecked eyes. "Just hold me!" she commanded. Jonny took her in her arms in a flash. He kissed her. Eventually he said, "Oh sweetheart, I don't care if it takes the rest of my life, but I promise I'll make it up to you. Now come here, we've got a lot of making up to do."
Shady wagged her tail. Sarah looked at Jonny and they both laughed. It was going to be all right. They leant in to kiss again just as the phone rang.
The smile on Jonny's face drained away as he listened to a frantic Suzy. Amy had been kidnapped.

Amy skipped along quite happily until the rain started. She wondered where her nanny Joycie was. She would have brought her umbrella, she was sure of it. Nanny Joycie never forgot things like that. She would have brought her lovely pink raincoat too, the nice new coat her mummy had bought for her. She wished she had her wellies on. She would have loved to jump and splash in the puddles. She loved to do that with Lydia. She was supposed to be with Lydia now. She was very wet. Her hair was dripping down her neck. She shivered. She had her school cardigan on, but it was soaked through. She was very cold and had goose pimples. She could hear her teeth chattering. Her hair was plastered to her head and nanny Violet was acting very funny. She had been all right at first.
She had told her she was taking her to see her mummy Suzy, and Amy had been happy to go along. They had headed towards Chapel Market where her mummy worked. They had gone along Moreland Street and turned into City Road. Amy knew this route. She walked it often with her mum or nanny Joycie. Sometimes they walked straight up City Road towards the Angel station. If it was a sunny day, they might go along by the canal if they were going to see Lydia. They were down by the canal now. Amy had never been here in the rain. She liked the way the raindrops splashed onto the water and she loved seeing the brightly painted narrow boats. At first, it had been fun. Then Amy had realised that she was hungry and she was very cold now. Nanny Violet did not seem to know Amy was with her anymore. She kept calling her Ellie May. "I'm not Ellie May, silly!" Amy had said the first time she had said

it. Amy knew that Ellie May was her big sister. Her mummy had told her all about Ellie May. She kept a picture of her on top of the telly at home. Amy kissed it every night before going to bed. Ellie May had gone to heaven a long time ago. Nanny Violet would not listen though. She had let go of Amy's hand and was sitting on the sopping wet bench singing to herself. "Nanny Vi, I'm cold. Can we go home now please? I want my mum."
Violet looked at her blankly. "Billy? Is that you? Put the kettle on, there's a good boy."
Amy hesitated, but only for a minute or two. She knew that nanny Violet wasn't very well. She wasn't supposed to cross the road on her own, but she knew where Lydia's house was. It was not very far from here. She ran along the canal towpath and up the stairs. Lydia's mummy would know what to do.

As Jay opened the door onto the street, Jonny Mason pulled up. An anguished Sarah pulled open the car door. Jon wound down the window and said, "Jay, hop in. Wherever you're going, I'll take you." Robert and Bob Pond were just behind Jay. Jay nodded gratefully at Jonny and turning to Robert and Bob said, "Okay, you two go together, and we'll go in Jon's car. We can meet back here in an hour. If Suzy's right and Violet has taken Amy, chances are she will take her to her flat. We'll go towards the Packington Estate first." Sarah waited until the car pulled away then ran into the flats to try to comfort Suzy.
As Jonny pulled away from the curb, he said, "I think we might as well park the car outside my house and then search on foot around the Packington Estate. We'll be able to see a lot more that way."
Jay nodded. He scrutinised the street as they drove along, his eyes searching for his little girl.

Jon parked the car in the street outside his house in Duncan Terrace. Before he had switched off the engine, Jay had opened the door and was running across the road. "Amy! Amy!"
A bedraggled Amy spotted her father from the public gardens opposite the house. Her little face lit up in delight and she ran and flung herself into Jay's arms. He took his jacket off and wrapped it around his

shivering daughter. "Oh boy, am I glad to see you!" he said with great understatement.

"I knocked and knocked at Lydia's door, but no one answered." Amy said, winding her arms around Jay's neck. He lifted her up and hugged her to him. "That's because everyone's out looking for you, sweetheart, even the police." Amy's eyes widened like saucers.

"Oh. Am I in trouble, dad?" Jay smiled and kissed her nose. They had reached the car and Jonny grabbed a blanket from the back seat. Jay took it gratefully and wrapped Amy in it as he helped her in. He settled himself next to her and said softly "No darling, you're not in any trouble. You can tell me what happened on the way home. I think Mummy has waited long enough to see you. Let's get cracking."

CHAPTER ELEVEN

Jay kissed Suzy and hugged Amy tightly. Bobby Jay was still at the table happily eating his breakfast of boiled egg and soldiers. He waved an eggy piece of bread at his daddy and smiled. Jay grinned. "You're meant to eat it BJ, not wave it. It's not a flag you know." Little Bobby Jay giggled and took a big bite of his soldier. Suzy winked at Jay as she wiped Bobby Jay's egg smeared face. "Go on, you get off. We'll be fine, honest love"

Jay was reluctant to go off to work. It was such a relief to have his family all together again but he was terrified to let them out of his sight. He watched Amy now as she chatted to her little brother at the table. He loved them all so much. Amy was safe and seemed to be none the worse for her unfortunate mishap. He had been trying to play down his anxiety in front of Suzy and the kids. Suzy was so ecstatic to see Amy's safe return she had not stopped smiling. She had checked and double checked with the school however, reassuring herself that no one picked up Amy without permission. She did not want to scare Amy and turn into a neurotic mother but she could not help but be cautious. They had been so apologetic at the school and had told her that they had looked into their security measures very thoroughly. They stressed that nothing like the unfortunate incident would ever happen again. They were talking to the board of governors about installing surveillance cameras in the playground by all the entrances and exits, and meanwhile the school caretaker had strict instructions not to unlock the gates at home time until the bell had gone for the end of the school day. In future, the parents would collect the children straight from the classrooms, which opened onto the school playground. This would ensure that no strangers could take children from the crowded playground unseen. Any unauthorised people would be questioned, and if in any doubt, they would not be allowed to take a child until their identity had been verified. Supply teachers would no longer be in charge of classes unless a qualified teaching assistant known to the children was also present. All staff members would in future wear identification with their photographs clearly visible. It all sounded very reassuring, but Suzy was still edgy. She tried to remain calm in front of Jay, however. She knew how worried he was about all of them after their ordeal.

Suzy had told poor Joycie and Carrie that they were not to blame. They had both been beside themselves and wracked with guilt. Suzy had done her best to tell them it had just been a fluke and an unfortunate set of circumstances. They had both been blaming themselves for being a few minutes late. The police had been round to let them know that Violet had been found. She had been wet through from all the heavy rain but otherwise unharmed. The police had found her sitting on a bench, still down by the canal where Amy had left her. Her poor husband, Don had been frantic. He had called the police to alert them that she had gone missing. Violet had recently gone into a care home at Finchley but had somehow managed to wander off and get on a bus all the way back to Islington. All the loose ends had been tied up, or so it seemed. All except one. Martin Crayford was still out there somewhere.

Carrie sat at her kitchen table. Sarah had just made her a cup of tea. She had brought Lydia to see her straight from school. Since Amy had gone missing, Sarah and Suzy were taking it in turns to leave the shop early and pick up the girls themselves. Joycie and Carrie had been mortified when they had first suggested it, both feeling that their daughters no longer trusted them to care for their granddaughters. Sarah had been quick to point out that they would trust them with their lives if need be, but they felt guilty for taking advantage. Sarah kept apologising, saying she should never have left Carrie to look after Lydia so soon after her health scare. "Don't be so daft" Carrie had said to Sarah, patting her hand. "You know what I'm like. I always want to be useful, and I insisted. I'm so sorry I let you down"

"Oh mum, don't! You've never let me down, not ever. I should never have taken advantage of you. I've not been fair." Back and forth they went, each apologising and berating themselves. They had eventually come to a compromise, and now shared the responsibility. Now they had become used to the new routine, Carrie had to admit that she had been finding things before a bit tiring. She realised she had taken on too much too soon in her eagerness to prove that she was once again fit and raring to go. Lydia was a delightful child and Carrie had recovered well from her operation. However, she did get tired and sometimes

150

enjoyed just putting her feet up in the afternoons and maybe even having a little nap. She loved it when Sarah dropped in, though. Lydia was now in the next room, happily watching her favourite cartoon on telly. Sarah dipped a rich tea biscuit into her tea. Carrie put a hand on her daughters arm and patted it lovingly. "I'm so glad you and Jonny have made it up and got back together. You look like your old self again, darling." She said, her eyes smiling. Sarah's own eyes widened in surprise. She dropped her rich tea biscuit into her cup. She had tried so hard to keep the truth from her mother. She had been terrified that the stress and worry would bring on another heart attack. Carrie laughed when she saw Sarah's expression. She watched her trying to retrieve the soggy bits from her teacup. "You needn't look so surprised, love. I always could read you like a book. I knew something wasn't right, I've been worried about you for ages. I just didn't like to ask. I was sure it was all my fault. You know me and my big gob, going on about the bloody secret when I was out of my head on painkillers in that hospital. I should never have said anything." She lowered her voice and said in a whisper, "Lydia let it slip that you and Jon had split up. She told me she liked Uncle Adam, but she was so glad that you were all back together again."

Nina sat on Adam's sofa. She felt a bit uncomfortable. It was the first time she had been round to his flat since she had admitted to herself that she fancied the pants off him. Now she had come clean, at least to herself, she did not know how to look Adam in the eye. He had invited her around for a Friday night takeaway. Nina was enjoying a rare evening off. She had all weekend off, in fact.
"Are you all right my little chickpea?" Adam said jovially as he handed Nina a much-needed glass of wine. "Sorry it's only cheap muck. Not up to your posh hotel standards, but it all goes down the same way." He added cheerfully, slumping down beside her. "You're very quiet tonight." He went on, prodding her with an elbow. She was very aware of his nearness. He smelled quite wonderful. She took a large glug of her wine to buy some time. Managing a grin, she said eventually, " Oi, careful. You nearly spilt my drink. It might only be cheap muck, but let's not waste it. Don't worry, I'm...fine. Just a bit tired that's all. She took another gulp of the wine. "Hmm, it's quite nice, actually. Moreish. It's

been a long week." She downed the rest of her glass in one more greedy mouthful and poured some more. Adam was eyeing her suspiciously. It was very disconcerting. She avoided his eyes. Her wine glass had suddenly become fascinating. Adam seemed to be enjoying her discomfort, but she could have been imagining it.

"Well, if you're sure." He said, noncommittally. He took a large gulp from his own glass. "Shall we order some grub? I only managed to grab half a sandwich for lunch today. I didn't even get to have my elevenses with Sarah and Suze. I only got to pop my head round the door for a few seconds. They've threatened mutiny. It was my turn to supply the donuts. I had to deal with a disgruntled stall owner. They can turn very nasty when roused." He grinned and added, "If enough customers poke 'em with sticks, they bite." He got up and rifled through a kitchen drawer until he found a dog eared menu. "What do you fancy?" Nina was sure he raised his eyebrows at that last remark. He held out the menu for her to look at. She pretended not to notice his expression, and avoided his eyes again.

"I'll have my usual. Egg fried rice, Sweet and sour chicken, no pineapple please." Nina said after giving the menu a once over to hide her embarrassment. "Boringly predictable, but I do love a bit of sweet and sour." She added. Was she babbling? What was wrong with her? It was Adam, for goodness sake. They were just mates. She didn't want to ruin a perfectly good friendship by getting all soppy. It would complicate things, and she had already had enough complications in her life. She thought of Nico. Thinking of him did not make her heart contract anymore. What did that mean? What did Adam mean to her? She tried to imagine her life without Adam in it and the thought made her feel panicky. She told herself off. She was just being stupid. Besides, she was sure that Adam still carried a torch for Sarah. She had seen the way he looked at her often enough. Even worse than imagining him with Sarah, she imagined how she would feel if Adam found himself a girlfriend. The thought made her feel murderous.

Adam duly noted down her food request. "Crackers?" he said, looking up from his pad and biro.

"I think I must be" Nina said without thinking. She was still busy thinking of Adam locked in an embrace with some harlot. Adam roared with laughter and managed to splutter, "I meant prawn crackers, nitwit."

Nina had to join in with the laughter. She managed to shake her head to decline eventually.

He picked up the telephone when he had stopped laughing and ordered their food. After he had sat down again, Nina said tentatively, "I expect you're missing Sarah now she has gone back home?" Adam nodded. Despite herself, she felt her spirits plummet.

Yeah, of course, I miss her and little Lydia but I'm glad they saw sense. Sarah and Jonny, I mean. "They are made for each other. Little Lydia's got more sense than the pair of them put together." He grinned. He was very fond of Lydia she was a great kid. She was as bright as a shiny new penny and they had some very deep meaningful conversations. Usually about whether Birds Eye Fish fingers were better than Findus. It had been heart breaking though, seeing her crying for her daddy. Sarah had felt awful about causing her baby girl such pain. She had been beside herself with guilt and Adam had been at a loss to know what to do or say to help. Lydia had also been pining for Shady the dog. Adam had said Shady could come to stay, but Sarah had reluctantly decided it wasn't fair for her to be left alone all day while they were at work. She usually stayed at home with Victor or Marlayna. She would go to the antique shop with Jonny if no one was at home all day. Poor Lydia cried for her dog every night. Sarah was reduced to tears, too. "Oh Adam, what am I doing?" she had sniffed one night. Adam had tried to comfort her, but he knew she had made the right decision when she said she had to try again with Jonny.

Nina was surprised by Adams attitude. He did not look in the least upset about Sarah going back to her husband again.

"I always thought you had a soft spot for Sarah. You must have had a twinge or two of jealousy?" She pressed. It was painful prying like this, but she had to know the truth.

Adam looked astonished. He had not realised that anyone knew how he had felt about Sarah. "Blimey, you don't miss a trick, do you?" he said, grinning again. That smile of his was a lethal weapon, Nina thought. Adam looked straight at Nina and went on honestly ,"Well, yes, in the beginning I did quite fancy Sarah, I have to confess. She is a beautiful woman, and such a lovely person. She always makes me laugh too, which is a huge plus point. But she is so in love with that husband of hers and I am nothing if not a gentleman. The last thing she needed was me making a move on her. It would've been easy to do, with her being so vulnerable after they split up. She badly needed a shoulder to cry on. I'm a decent bloke, believe it or not. I don't make a habit of taking advantage of my mates. That's all I ever was, a shoulder for her, you know. I'm not some leering lecherous dribbling fool waiting to pounce on any unsuspecting woman who feels a tad upset."

Nina couldn't help smiling. He really was lovely. "I'm sorry; I should keep my big fat nose out of it. I just wondered that's all." She topped up her drink. She couldn't remember when she had needed a drink more.

"Not a problem. Besides, I've got someone else in mind now." Nina nearly dropped her wine glass.

"Oh?" she managed to squeak, "Anyone I know?" Adam looked her in the eye. She tried to turn away, but he would not let her. He gently turned her face towards him. His eyes studied her face. "Yes, you, you daft old bat!" he said softly. "I might just take advantage of you, if you've got no objections. If you're not still on the rebound that is."

"Oh no I've rebound and bounced right back." Nina whispered, smiling at him. He hesitated for a moment, giving her time to stop him, and then leaned in. Nina felt her heart pound and closed her eyes expectantly, waiting for their first kiss.

The doorbell made them both jump. They burst out laughing. It was their takeaway. That kiss would have to keep.

"I feel huge!" Sarah said to Suzy. "I don't remember being this big when I carried Lyddy. Look at the size of my bum. It needs its own postcode!" Suzy laughed. She finished dusting the shelves and climbed down from her stool. "Rubbish, you look radiant. Especially since you got back with Jon. You've got a real twinkle in your eye, and a lovely neat little bump. You look glowing. Now, I was enormous when I carried Bobby Jay. You could've landed a helicopter on my arse!" They both giggled. "How are things between you two? I know I shouldn't say anything, but hell, I'm going to. I'm so glad you saw sense." Sarah looked up in surprise.

"What do you mean, saw sense? If you saw a naked picture of your Jay that another woman had taken, you'd have chopped his balls off and hung them out to dry!"

"Well, yes, that's true. Believe me though, I can smell a bastard a mile off. I've had plenty of practise, but your Jonny is a good un. He was lost without you, and you were in bits. Don't deny it, cos I know you too well. You two were meant for each other. That bloody cow Louise is a born troublemaker. You can't believe a word she says. Don't ever let her come between you two again."

"Do you think she meant what she said about it being all lies and that she was sorry? I can't stop thinking about it." Sarah said with a worried expression on her face. "I want to believe Jon, and I know deep down I can trust him, but...well, there's still a little voice inside my head that says what if?"

"Well, I don't know if she is sorry, but I'm sure she was lying about everything else. Your Jon would never cheat on you. I'd bet my life on it. He loves the bones of you. Anyway, who cares whether she is sorry or not? It don't matter now, does it? You two are hunky dory again, and if she ever pops up round here, you can rip her bloody head off, and I'll help yer."

"Blimey, I hope she doesn't show up again. I hope she moves back to the wilderness with that poor hubby of hers where she belongs and never shows her face round here again. What a complete bitch she is. It's that poor husband I feel sorry for."

"Never mind about her! What about you and Jon? Are you shagging each other's brains out to make up for all that lost time?" she nudged Sarah's arm teasingly. Sarah turned a delicate shade of beetroot red, as Suzy knew she would. "Come on; tell me all the dirty details"
Sarah giggled and blushed even more. "Sod off you nosy mare."

Camilla waited impatiently outside the hospital oncology unit. Louise had promised faithfully to meet her there. She had sworn that she would never let her down ever again, and offered her unswerving support. Camilla looked at her watch again. She had tried ringing her, both at the Barbican flat and at her father's house, but there had been no reply. Camilla could not hang around hoping she would turn up any longer. If she did not go inside now she would be late for her appointment. Furiously she opened the double doors of the long corridor and walked along to the reception area. She cursed herself for daring to trust Louise. She had actually believed she had changed. She might have known that Louise would let her down as usual.

Simon Collier whistled to his dog Jess. She had disappeared into the undergrowth and was digging excitedly, sending dirt and leaves everywhere. "Aww, leave her, she's having a lovely time. There's no one around. Give us a kiss," his girlfriend Claire said. Simon smiled and leant down to kiss Claire's upturned face. They often walked the dog through Highgate woods. It was the only chance they had to be alone. Simon pulled Claire closer to him and kissed her harder. He pushed her gently up against an obliging tree and began to caress her breasts. She moaned appreciatively and ran her fingers deliciously down his spine. Then Jess began barking loudly. They both laughed and Simon said, "Where would we be without our passion killer?" he reluctantly pulled away from Claire and looked over to where the dog was still digging and barking frantically now. His eyebrows knotted in concern.
"What is it girl?" they walked closer to Jess who had appeared covered in leaves and was wagging her tail and wiggling with excitement. The dog ran back to the spot she had been digging at.
Simon bent down to look under the bushes, but it was Claire's piercing screams that told him she had spotted it first.
A human arm was sticking out of the dirt.

Detective Inspector William Paisley rubbed his tired eyes. He looked up at the clock on his office wall. His shift should have finished an hour ago but he had become lost in paperwork as usual. His desk was littered with his latest case file and empty coffee cups. He was dying for a cigarette, and he felt his stomach rumble with hunger. He let out a puff of air and ran his fingers through his thick wavy hair. It was grey now at the temples but at least he still had a full head of hair he told himself. He let his eyes go back to the report in front of him. A courting couple out with their dog had found the body of a young woman in Highgate woods. She had been identified as Mrs Louise Bingly Warrington. The husband was a barrister, and the pair was resident in Shropshire. The woman had been staying in London though, nursing her sick mother. The husband claimed to be in Shropshire at the time of his wife's death. The father still lived in the parental home, not far from where the body had been discovered. The father had appeared to be beside himself with grief. He had recently lost his wife, and now his only child was dead. She had been murdered. Death by strangulation. The pathology report had stated someone tall had killed the woman, over six feet judging by the position of the bruising around her neck. The killer had used his bare hands to asphyxiate her. Paisley threw a ball of paper expertly through his office door to grab the attention of his constable, Mark Davis as he went past. It hit his target.

"Davis, in here! I want you to go with Seargent Dukes to do some house to house enquiries first thing in the morning. I need you both working with me on this babe in the woods case. She was a local girl. Someone must have seen or heard something. Also, let's get the husband in again. Find out where he really was around the estimated time of death. Make sure he doesn't bugger off back to Shropshire until we've got the bastard who did this. Look up everyone in her address book and pay them a call too. Her handbag was found at the scene of the crime, Her purse, address book and house keys were still inside it. Oh, and I want another word with her father. Let's get this one wrapped up as soon as possible. I want to know what sort of a woman she was, who her friends were, who she was knobbing behind hubby's back. They had plenty of money by all accounts. The father is an antique dealer. He's got a big house, and a shop in Highgate Village or Hampstead. Check it out. The husband's family owns half of ruddy Shropshire. Those rich types get up to all sorts. See if they've got anything to hide. Be discrete, Davis. I don't want that wanker from The Daily Mail sniffing round again. I want the bastard that did this nailed to my wall, and I don't want any buggers from the paper telling me how to do my job." He pointed at the file on his desk and took out his packet of cigarettes. It was empty and he cursed loudly, crushing the packet in his hands and tossing it viciously into the bin. "Take this file, go home and get yourself up to speed, oh, and tell Dukes to do the same. "

Don Jameson sat in the day room beside his wife Violet. He came to see her every day but he sometimes wondered why he still bothered. She had no idea who he was anymore and the visits broke his heart. He could not bear to see her visibly fading before his eyes. She was like an ice block melting in the heat of the sun. Every day now, she was shrinking farther and farther away from him. Soon there would be nothing left of the person he had married all those years ago. He was a gruff sort of man, not one to show his emotions but he had loved Violet with all his heart when they married. He had been faithful too. He had no time for womanising. He had worked hard all his life and had been proud to bring his wage packet home to his wife and family. Things had been all right, they had been happy until the boys came along. His sons were a disappointment to him he had to admit. Violet had always been saddened by his attitude towards his children, and it had caused a rift between them. His younger son Graham had always tried hard, but had never amounted to anything much. As for the other one, Billy, well he was a total waste of space. Still, they had jogged along together and he could not imagine life without Violet in it. They had driven each other mad over the years but having no one to complain about was a daunting prospect.

Jane, the care assistant brought him a cup of tea and interrupted his thoughts. He took it gratefully. She smiled at him. "Are you all right there, Don?" she said cheerfully. He looked up at her bright young face. She was always cheerful and he envied her. Life had not yet weighed her down with its inevitable sorrows. He sighed wearily. "Not really, love."

Violet was humming to herself. Jane made sure Violet was comfortable then turned to Don again. She touched his arm gently as he put down his teacup.

"I know it can be difficult." She said kindly, "But even though she doesn't know you, you know her. Cling on to the happy memories of the person you loved. That will be a comfort to you one day."

Don managed a half smile. "I hope you're right love." He said sadly. "Those memories from years ago are all I've got left now"

CHAPTER TWELVE

Suzy had gone over to the bakers to get their morning cake order. The sun was out and it looked like it was going to be a nice warm day. She ordered the cakes and chatted happily to Gill the assistant. She carefully put the deliciously naughty items into the white cardboard box. Gill handed Suzy her change and the cake box. She had worked in the bakers for over twenty years and had known Suzy since she was a little girl. "Tata love. See yer tommorer." she said as Suzy turned to leave. "Bye Gill. Thanks."

When Suzy crossed the road and went into the shop, Sarah was nowhere to be seen. The shop was empty. It had been quiet today, very few customers were out and about in the market yet but Sarah would never leave the shop unattended. "Hello!" Suzy called out nervously, heading for the back room. "Sarah, are you there?"

"I'm in here! Come quick!" came Sarah's distressed voice from the small staff toilet. Suzy put the cake box down hurriedly and rushed to the toilet door. She banged loudly on the wood and Sarah pulled the bolt across and pushed it open.

"My waters have broken!" she gasped. She was bent double over the hand basin. Suzy looked aghast at her friends pain wracked face and realised in an instant that her labour pains had obviously started too. "Oh bloody 'ell!" Suzy said none too diplomatically. The baby was not due for another six weeks.

"Call a ruddy ambulance!" Sarah said through gritted teeth, then added, "And get Jon!"

Jonny had never been in an interview room at a police station before. He hoped he would never have to be in one ever again, either. He had been really shocked when two police officers had turned up at the shop and asked him to accompany them to the police station. They had said they would like him to help with their enquiries into the murder of Louise Bingly Warrington. He was still reeling from the news. Louise had been murdered! He had been happy to help, but he had been in this room for hours now. They had asked him hundreds of questions and Jon was horrified to realise that he was actually a suspect. He had told them everything he knew, from the last time he had seen her to when they had first met. He had a tight knot of fear in his stomach. He wondered if they were going to arrest him.

Suzy helped Sarah into the ambulance. They had quite an audience. All the stall holders were goggling at them and where had all the blooming shoppers suddenly appeared from? It had been like a ghost town ten minutes ago, Suzy thought peevishly. She had not been able to get hold of Jonny either. He was not picking up on his shop phone. She had left a message on the answer phone.

She had managed to speak to Victor at their home number and he had promised that he would meet Sarah at the hospital. "Are you sure you don't want me to come with you?" Suzy said again anxiously. Sarah shook her head. "No, stay and look after the shop, Suze, but please get my mum and keep trying Jon. Where the bloody hell is he?"

Robert got back to the shop after his delivery round and found Suzy nervously drumming her fingers on the counter. She looked up crossly at her brother. "What's up with you, face ache?" Robert teased. "Oh Rob, Sarah's gone into labour. It's way too early and I can't get hold of Jonny. I've been ringing and ringing but he never answers the bloody thing. I've got three more deliveries for you, sorry. They came in at the last minute and all of them want delivery today." Suzy slumped back on her stool. "Oh, and there's an apple donut for you in the back room if you want one."

Robert smiled at his sister. She had said everything in a rush and now looked as if her batteries had run out. "Okay, easy, tiger." He quipped, "I'll give you a lift to the hospital if you want. Is she at the U.C.H?" Suzy nodded. "Her mum's with her. Carrie rang me just now. Sarah's just been taken down to the delivery room. This baby is going to be born and nothing can stop it. Poor little mite, he or she is going to be very premature. Where the hell could Jonny have got to? He should be there with her. Thanks for the offer of a lift, Rob. Sorry, I know I'm waffling on. I always get verbal diarrhoea when I'm nervous. I won't go to the hospital just yet. I just want to get home to Jay and the kids. I'm gonna shut up shop a bit early. I'll go later when I've got them settled. One of the deliveries is in Turnpike house, so if you can drop me off I'll do that one and then I can walk home."

"Are you sure?"

"Yeah, I can pick Amy up from school. It's just next door to the flats where the delivery is. The delivery should only take me a few minutes. You can get off and do the others and then go home. Mums got Bobby Jay. I'll pop in to see her and wait for further news. I'll go up to the hospital and see Sarah later. They won't want me hanging around while she's still in labour anyway. I'll wait for a bit. Victor said they'd ring as soon as they know anything. Hopefully, it will be good news. "

Martin Crayford had been busy over the last few weeks. He had had lot of arrangements to make. He had fled after Adele had whacked him round the head. He did not blame her, not really. He had scared her, he realised that now. She had cut his head quite badly with that fucking frying pan, but he had not wanted to risk going to hospital. He had patched himself up as best as he could. He was fine. He had a cast iron scull after all the boxing he had done. It had not been easy dodging the police, or finding out about Jay fucking Oakland and his family. The filth were still looking for him. He got a kick out of knowing that he was one step ahead of the plods, though. Here he was, right under their bloody noses. They had even been to his lock up garage in Jaywick. He wouldn't make the mistake of going near there again. He knew they had been sniffing around. They had moved everything, the stupid twats. They had to have found out about that from that nosy bastard Oakland. Martin had been mildly surprised that he had remembered about the garage. Well, he wasn't the only one who had a good memory. He remembered Dennis telling Adele about Oakland's wife and kids. He had even met Oakland's wife once, at that school fete. She was a real looker too. She had been helping out on one of the pathetic little stalls. Another do gooder. Martin knew a lot of people in Islington, he had friends here and he had done some sniffing around. He had enjoyed the detective work and the planning, and the game of cat and mouse. He was smarter than any of them. A lot smarter than that do gooding Jay Oakland any day. They would never find him. He was too audacious, he thought smugly.

He looked out of the bedroom window and watched the children in the school playground through his binoculars. He got a good view of the primary school from his friends flat in Turnpike house. Old Tony Mallory had not been too keen on letting him stay, but it was amazing what a bit of bribery could achieve. Besides, Martin knew a lot about Tony that he would rather keep to himself. If the police ever found out about his little stash of class A drugs in the wardrobe for instance, he would be in deep doggy doo doo. Tony sold a bit here and there to help keep the wolf from the door so he had reluctantly allowed his house guest to move in. Martin could be very persuasive with his fists and his threats.

Martin made himself comfortable by the bedroom window. He homed in on the pretty little dark haired girl. He knew now that she was Amy Oakland. He could not believe his fortitude when he saw her mother walking out of the school gates with the little girl skipping slightly ahead. He had not thought that he would get so lucky so quickly. He had been prepared to play the waiting game. He knew that Jay Oakland's brother in law usually did the deliveries from the shop where Jay's wife worked. He had hoped to find out a few snippets of information from the brother in law, but bingo, he had struck gold. He would get to meet little wifey again and the kid a lot sooner than he had dreamed. The wifey still looked like a tasty sort, too. She was carrying the gift basket that he had ordered. He had rung the shop and placed a delivery order under a false name of course. He had ordered some cheap shit just to get them here. He had seen the van with the shop name emblazoned on its side pull up, and watched her get out as it pulled up in the car park beside the flats. She had carried the basket with her into the school and waved to her little daughter. The van had driven off.

He could not wait for the basket to be delivered. He looked at the clock on Tony's bedside table. She would be knocking on the front door in five minutes maximum, he estimated. She was holding her little daughters hand now. He waited in anticipation. He had lost his wife and his stepson because of that interfering bastard Jay Oakland. Let's see how he likes it, he thought as he smiled to himself.

Jonny blinked as he came out of the police station and breathed in the fresh air. The sour faced detectives had finally said he was free to go. Jonny got the distinct impression that he had not seen the last of DC

Davis or Seargent Dukes. They had given Jonny a look that clearly said they did not believe a word of what he had told them. Hopefully, they would change their minds once they checked out all the information Jonny had given. He knew he had nothing to hide. What was it about Coppers ? They made you feel guilty even when you knew you had done nothing wrong. It made him feel sick though, knowing that whoever did kill poor Louise was still out there somewhere. He headed for a phone box to ring his dad. He had some explaining to do about why the shop was closed in the middle of the day. He also had to break the news about Louise. He felt awful knowing that he had said some terrible things to her the last time they had spoken. No matter how annoying she had been, she did not deserve to end up like that. He knew that Victor would want to be there for her father. That poor man, Jonny thought as he opened the door of the phone box. Greg had certainly been through it.

"Jon? Is that you? Oh thank God, where have you been?" It was Marlayna who had snatched up the phone on the first ring. She did not give Jonny any chance to reply. Instead she said urgently, "You must get to the hospital as soon as you can. Sarah went into premature labour."

Jay was surprised to see Joycie in his living room when he got home. "Hi Joyce" he began to say. Then he saw her worried face and he felt a knot grip his stomach. "What is it?" he said flatly.
"It's probably nothing," Joyce said quietly, trying to sound calm. Then she added, "Nobody has seen Suzy since she collected Amy from school"

Jay automatically scooped Bobby Jay up in his arms and kissed him as Joycie quickly explained everything. She knew that Suzy would not have gone straight to the hospital to be with Sarah without letting anyone know. Robert gave Jay the address that Suzy had gone to with the gift basket. Joycie had already rung the school and they had confirmed that Suzy had collected Amy at home time. No one had seen them since. Jay took a moment and looked across at Robert. "Let's go." he said simply, as he handed his son back to Joycie.

163

"You took your ruddy time!" Sarah said to a flustered Jonny when he finally walked into the delivery suite. He had been devastated when he got there to be met by Carrie. She had hastily told him that he had a son and the doctors had just finished tidying Sarah up after the birth. His father and Marlayna had just gone to get cups of tea for everyone. Lydia ran to Jonny and said excitedly "Daddy, I've got a baby brother. He's ever so little though, like one of my dollies. I only sawed him for a minute, and they took him to a special box to help him get bigger." Jonny scooped his lovely little daughter up in his arms and hugged her tight. "Oh darling, aren't we lucky? You'll make a smashing big sister. Now if you don't mind, I'd like to go and see mummy for a little while. Will you be a good girl and stay with Nana for a bit?" Carrie smiled at them both. "Go on. I think you're in for an earful. I'll leave you to it." Jonny smiled at Carrie as he put Lydia down. "Thanks" he said as he tentatively opened the door to the delivery suite.

"Where the hell have you been?" Sarah had added, as he sat down breathlessly. He could not believe he had missed his son's entrance to the world. "It's a long story. I'm so sorry." He leant over and kissed Sarah. To his relief, she did not press him further or pull away. She gave him a half smile and said softly, "Well, you can tell me later. Help me get up off this bed please. They're insisting I go in a wheelchair so you'll have to get one from the porter first. Then we can both go down to the premature baby unit and meet our son."

"I wish I could hold him. He looks so tiny." Sarah said tearfully to Jonny as they both gazed at their son. Jonny was quite overwhelmed. He was absolutely devastated that he had missed the birth of his child. The guilt swamped him and he could not speak. Sarah had told him on their way to the premature baby unit that he had been whisked away almost as soon as he had been delivered. She had not even held him in her arms yet. It had been a difficult birth. He swallowed hard to try to dislodge the lump in his throat and at last, he said, "Oh Sarah, I'd give anything to turn back the clock so I could have been here. I'll never forgive myself. I hope you'll let me explain later, but not just yet. Let's just enjoy our little boy. I can't believe it, we've got a son. He's gorgeous. What shall we call him, have you thought of any names?"

Sarah could not stop gazing at her baby. Her arms ached to hold him. Instead, she put her hand on the incubator and said quietly, "Yes, I've done nothing but think of names. If Suzy doesn't mind, I'd like to call him Elliot. You know, in memory...a sort of tribute to her Ellie May? What do you think?"

Jonny smiled. He looked at Sarah, beautiful as ever, looking uncomfortable in the wheelchair. She was still so fresh faced and her eyes shone with love and concern for the fragile new life she had just given birth to. Jonny thought his heart would burst with the emotion of it all. It had been quite a day. "I think Elliot Mason has quite a ring to it. I love it." Their eyes met and they smiled at each other. Then Sarah said, "Where is Suzy, anyway? I thought she'd be here by now?"

When the gloating face of Martin Crayford appeared round the door after Jay's frantic knocking, Jay Oakland was not surprised. He knew his instincts had been right. "Where are they? What have you done to my wife and child?" Jay demanded furiously, forcing his way in and barging past Crayford. Robert was not far behind him. Jay had told Robert that he was sure Martin Crayford had something to do with Suzy and Amy's disappearance. Robert had to agree. They had raced to the address in Turnpike House to check it out.

Martin Crayford laughed nastily at Jay's frantic appearance and Jay and Robert turned to face him. Jay looked murderous. Crayford stood in the hall and grinned at them both. Martin Crayford had deliberately allowed them to barge past him into the hallway of the small flat. "It's not nice is it, not knowing where your family are?" Crayford said teasingly. Jay was only inches away from this loathsome man. Too late, Jay spotted the large hunting knife in Martin Crayford's hand.

Robert opened the door to the living room and burst in. "Jesus!" he said, shocked to his core. He heard the scuffle behind him as Jay and Crayford fought in the hallway, but he ran across the room to help his sister and precious little niece.

On the shabby looking carpet, Suzy and a terrified Amy were bound and gagged. Robert immediately went to them and gently began to remove the duct tape covering their mouths. He had a penknife in his pocket and he tried to cut the electrical flex that bound their wrists and ankles. The flex around Suzy's ankles was knotted tightly but he had cut part way through Suzy's wrist and ankle ties when he spun round at the sound of Crayford's voice. "I wouldn't do that if I were you." Crayford said calmly. He had Jay in a headlock and was holding the hunting knife to his throat. He indicated to Robert to move away from Suzy and Amy. "Now, that's a sensible boy" he said condescendingly as Robert did as he was told. Amy had been struggling but she lay very still, when she heard Crayford's voice. Robert had almost cut through her bonds but she had her hands behind her back and Crayford could not tell she was free. Robert had put the penknife on the floor and Suzy had quickly put her feet on top of it to obscure it from Crayford's view.

He looked at Robert and said menacingly, "Put your hands where I can see them, and listen to what I have to say otherwise I'll slit his throat from ear to ear."

The knife at Jay's throat was pressing very tightly against his jugular vein and had actually begun to draw blood. It trickled down his neck and Jay saw Suzy's eyes bulge in terror. He tried to struggle but the grip on his throat was too tight. Martin Crayford was deceptively strong and he felt the scratch of the blade on his skin.

Crayford grinned when he saw the blood and looked over at Amy who was sobbing. "Oh dear little girl. Boo Hoo, am I hurting your precious daddy? Well shut the fuck up or I'll hurt him even more!"

"For Christ sake you bastard!" Robert screamed furiously, "What the fuck do you want? You sick moron, you're getting a kick out of frightening that little girl aren't you? Let Amy and Suzy go and we can sort this out whatever it is."

Maddeningly, Crayford laughed. "Shut up you fuckwit!" He said nastily. "I'll tell you what I want. I want my wife and my child back. That's all. Not much to ask, is it? I'll do a straight swap. If you tell me where Adele and Dennis are, I'll let you all go. If not, well, I've got nothing to lose, have I? I may as well slit all your throats! Or maybe I'll take that frightened little girl and dangle her over the balcony. Will that make you tell me where they are?" As he spoke, he gripped Jay's throat even tighter. Jay began to gag and the blade glinted in the light and drew more blood.

"Don't you dare hurt my Daddy!" Amy screamed as loudly as she could. Martin Crayford laughed loudly. "She's a feisty little thing, ain't she?" he

said, tightening his grip around Jay's throat again. "Shut your fucking trap you little bitch, or I'll kill him right now and you'll be next!"
Out of the corner of his eye, Robert noticed that Suzy had managed to free her hands from the electrical flex he had loosened. She kept them behind her back so that Crayford did not notice. She caught Robert's eye for a split second. He knew it was now or never. Robert saw the penknife just by her feet. He gave a barely audible nod to his sister. Crayford was not paying attention. He was looking at Jay. He was loving the sound of his own voice, and was on the biggest power trip he had ever been on. It was highly invigorating having this much control over people. He watched in fascination at the blood trickling down Jay's neck and spilling onto his own shirtsleeve.
He did not expect Suzy and Robert to rush at him together. Robert hit him in his midriff with the full force of his head. He was winded and his legs sagged. He still had his arm across Jay's neck, and as he fell, he pulled Jay down with him.
Suzy had yanked her feet apart from the ties, grabbed the penknife and managed to swing at Crayford's legs. She stuck the penknife into his calf with all the might she could muster. He screamed and kicked out. The full force of his boot hit Suzy on the chin, but he had dropped the hunting knife and loosened his grip on Jay's throat. Suzy fell backward, dazed.
In an instant, Jay turned and swung his fist, bringing Crayford crashing down to the floor. Robert sat on his back and shouted to Jay to get the electrical flex and tie him up. Jay moved as fast as he could and grabbed the roll of flex that Crayford had left lying on the carpet. They hog-tied the protesting Crayford so he could not move. They were all surprised when Amy came over and pulled Crayford's hair as hard as she could and smacked him for good measure.
Suzy managed a half smile at her brave little girl as she sat up. She was still dazed and bruised from the kicking, but she managed to crawl across the carpet. She grabbed the phone and dialled the police.

CHAPTER THIRTEEN

"My word, I can't take my eyes off you for a second, can I?" Sarah said after kissing her bruised and battered friend. Suzy grinned ruefully. She had finally managed to visit the hospital. She had just finished telling Sarah all about the drama that had occurred. She was still a little shell shocked, but so relieved it was all over and that they were all safe. Amy was busy telling an awe struck Lydia all about her adventure, and Lydia was listening spell bound as Amy told her friend all about how brave she and her mummy, daddy and uncle had been. She had shown off the bruises around her wrists and ankles where Crayford had tied her up. Suzy could not bear to look. She worried what long term harm that monster had caused her precious little girl. She could not help chuckling though as she listened to Amy's tale getting taller by the minute. She said to her daughter gently, "Amy, don't exaggerate. That bad man did not have a machine gun, or laser beams for eyes."

Amy looked sheepish. Suzy and Jay exchanged grins and tried not to laugh aloud. She seemed to be coping well so far. "Well, he nearly did. He was nasty to my daddy, but daddy was ever and ever so brave. Uncle Robert and Mummy rushed at him, and Daddy bashed him too. I helped. I smacked him and pulled his horrible hair. Then the police came, there were thousands of them.." she looked back at Suzy who had raised her eyebrows. "Well, there were lots anyway, and they are locking him up for always. He won't be able to hurt us anymore now. My Daddy said so."

Jay and Suzy exchanged glances again. Jay winked reassuringly at Suzy. He had a dressing on his neck where Crayford had cut him but was otherwise unscathed. Physically at least. They had all given statements to the police and had had their injuries photographed and been seen by a doctor. It was good to get back to normality. The whole episode now felt like a very bad dream.

They had watched the police the day before handcuff and lead away the struggling Martin Crayford. It had been blatantly obvious that the man was unhinged. Jay had not cared that the man had mental health problems. He had no sympathy for the brute. He had tried to hurt his family and he hoped the police would lock him up in a secure unit and throw away the key.

His eyes had been crazed and something had died inside them. It had made Suzy's flesh creep just to look at him. She had cuddled her precious little girl to her chest and felt her frightened child's heart beating as loudly as her own. She heard her brother Robert saying quietly to Crayford, "I hope they lock you up for the rest of your life you crazy bastard!"

Jay had hugged Suzy and Amy. He had tried to calm them down, and reassure them that he was fine. Blood had been seeping down his neck though and an officer had had to attend his wound. They had heard the wail of sirens as an ambulance had arrived. Jay had needed three stitches but luckily, the knife had not pierced any major arteries or caused any permanent damage. Suzy had clung to Jay and Amy had clung to them both. Robert, bless him had been the practical one and had found cotton wool in the bathroom for the officer to clean and dress Jay's neck.

It had seemed very quiet once Crayford had been bundled outside. They sat together, waiting for the ambulance to arrive, united again as a family.

Suzy hugged Sarah. Sarah had left the others to chat amongst themselves and had taken Suzy down to the premature baby unit. They looked at the sleeping baby in his Perspex box and Suzy's heart turned over. He was such a tiny little mite. It brought a lump to her throat seeing him wired up to the bleeping machines. Sarah put her hand through the little opening and the baby gripped her finger. She beamed in delight. "Oh Suze, look at him!" she said excitedly. "My lovely little boy. He is so titchy, but so perfect. He's a little fighter, too. The nurses say he's doing ever so well. I can't wait to hold him."

The baby loosened his grip on Sarah's finger and she gently stroked his arm. Then she turned to Suzy and said quietly, "Suze, do you mind, we want to call him Elliot, to honour Ellie May? Will it be painful to you if we call him Elli for short?"

Suzy could not speak. She was so overwhelmed and thrilled. She managed a smile. Eventually she said softly, "Mind? I think it's bloody

fantastic. Elliot Mason. What a grand name for a tiny tot. I love it, and Ellie May would have, too."
The baby slept peacefully as the two friends hugged again.

"Are you okay, Suze? You look tired," Sarah said, her face creased with concern. She had popped in to see Suzy at the shop. She was still on maternity leave, but she always tried to pop in before going to the hospital. She wanted to tell Suzy the good news that baby Elliot was finally coming home. The doctors had telephoned that morning and had told her and Jonny that he was strong enough at last. It had been two long months since his arrival. Sarah and Jonny had been visiting every day and could not wait to be a normal family at last. They were going to fetch him this very afternoon. "Yeah, I'm okay." Suzy said, stifling a yawn. "Just didn't get much sleep last night. Amy is still having nightmares about that bastard Crayford. She slept in our bed again last night. Bobby Jay woke up too." She smiled ruefully, then added, "At least there's no chance of me ever having any more kids. Chance would be a fine thing! I'm a bit worried about next door, too. You know Narky won't be coming back? He has to go into a care home. I can't bear the thought of getting squatters in there again. Anyway, how's Elliot? Is he still gaining weight?" Sarah beamed.
"He most certainly is. Guess what? He's coming home today!"
The door opened and Adam came in to see the two of them hugging and jumping up and down in delight. "What have I missed?" He said, "Is there a discount on donuts today?" Suzy let go of Sarah and they both turned and smiled at Adam. "Oh it's way better than that," Sarah said, grinning at Adam. "Little Elliot's coming home today!" Adam joined in the grinning. "Aw, that's fantastic. I'd say this calls for a celebration. I'll go and get us all some cream cakes and a bottle of something sparkly."

Detective Inspector Paisley looked again at the pathology report and forensic evidence on the babe in the woods case. He had hoped to have it all wrapped up by now, but they had still not arrested anyone. He had just had the wanker from the press on the phone again. He would kill Gill Evans on the bloody desk. Why the hell had she put that bastard through? She was a young officer who had so far shown a lot of promise, and he was disappointed in her. His phone was probably

170

broken now he had slammed it down so hard. The hacks were baying for blood, and he knew he could not hold them off for much longer. He opened his door and bellowed at Dukes. "I've just had Giles wanker Ogilvy on the blower! Tell Gill Evans to get her scrawny arse in here! Is she as dozy as she looks? I told her last week not to put any press calls through! How the fucking hell did he manage to smarm his way in?" He looked at the files on his desk. He had spoken to Dean Lauder in pathology for the umpteenth time. They must have missed something. He read the report again. The position of the bruising around the victim's neck indicated that the perpetrator of this particular crime was tall, probably over six feet. They had been told this since day one. They had spoken to every one they could who had even the vaguest connection to Louise Bingly Warrington now. Every six footer in a sixty mile bloody radius. He was desperate enough to start interviewing dwarves now. They had ruled out the women that Louise knew. Particularly the ones she had seriously pissed off. It seemed the victim had managed to piss off a lot of people. Sarah Mason in particular had reason to hate Mrs Bingly Warrington. However, she was petite, five foot five if that. She had also been very pregnant at the time Louise was killed. Louise's friend, Camilla was five foot seven. However, she had been receiving treatment for cervical cancer and would not have had the strength to overpower a struggling Louise. She had put up quite a fight. The husband, Rupert, was a prime suspect. He was six foot three but he had a cast iron alibi. He had been in his office in Shropshire at the time of death. He had several witnesses who had seen him there. He had even been spotted on a CT camera when he visited his local bank during his lunch hour. Unless he had a bloody Tardis like Doctor Who, there was no way he could have been in two places at once. The police had spoken again to Jon Mason. He was five feet eleven. It was still feasible he could have done it. Paisley shook out a cigarette and lit it. He sucked in his cheeks and took a huge drag and exhaled smoke all over the paperwork. He looked again. He was becoming more and more frustrated. He knew the answer was there somewhere. Louise had told quite a few porkie pies, so it was difficult to get to the truth. She had claimed that she had been having an affair with Jon Mason. She had a naked photograph of him, and her husband Rupert had told the police that she also claimed that he had given her two little teddy bears as love tokens. They had questioned Jon Mason for hours about it. He had told them he had been blind drunk on the night the photo was taken. Louise had apparently bundled him into a cab and all but abducted him. They had checked out his story, and managed to find the cab driver. He had confirmed that Mason had indeed been paralytic. As for the teddy bears, Mason had been able to produce receipts for the purchase of them by Louise herself. The silly woman had even written out a cheque which the bank had confirmed. Everything that Jon Mason had told them in his earlier interview had checked out. He had been telling the truth. Something was niggling at him though. He took another drag from his cigarette and riffled through the papers on his desk. Was that Jon Mason too good to be true? He came across as an extremely affable, likeable person, and he had been friendly and cooperative. Was he too amenable? He had a beautiful wife who he obviously loved to bits. Kids, too. He had a strong motive for wanting Louise out of the picture. She had caused him and his perfect little family nothing but trouble. Maybe it was time to pull him in again.

Gill Evans knocked nervously on the door. "Come in!"

Police constable Evans tried not to wrinkle her nose as the cigarette smoke hit her nostrils. She hated smokers. The office reeked of stale tobacco and coffee. She hated coffee too. Detective Inspector Paisley was an intimidating man but Gill Evans had the greatest respect for him, despite his nasty smoking habit. She had had to put up with many things that offended her senses since joining the force. She had soon learned how to ignore it after dealing with the first drunk who had puked all over her on a Friday night. Behind his gruff exterior and often politically incorrect manner was a dedicated, highly intelligent man who had shown her a lot of kindness. He had told her she showed great potential, and she longed to become a permanent member of his Major Incident team. She was fed up with answering phones and making tea. On a good day, she was allowed the responsibility of directing the traffic. That was not what she had joined the force to do. Paisley had once bellowed at her and told her that she was not Cagney or Lacey, and she had to serve her time before she got a taste of the interesting cases. "It took me fifteen years to become an overnight success," he had said scathingly. She had wearily taken his words on board, and

172

prepared to knuckle down and make a lot of tea and breathe in a lot of traffic fumes.

She appreciated Paisley singling her out, especially as she was one of the few female officers in this station. She could have kicked herself for letting that twat from the papers fool her. She hoped she had not blotted her copy book too much. "What have you got to say for yourself?" Paisley growled.

"I'm really sorry sir. I didn't recognise Ogilvy's voice. The bastard got someone else to ring at first and he told me he was a witness to the babe in the woods case. He insisted he had urgent information for you. He was adamant he would only speak to you sir." She noticed all the paper that littered the D.I's desk. "Sir?" she said nervously. "Yeah, what is it?" Paisley growled again, not looking up from his work. His cigarette was burning away neglected by Paisley, almost singeing his fingers.

"Well, it's probably nothing, but I have been following the babe in the woods case very closely and I couldn't help noticing..." Paisley looked up. "Well, Louise was found buried in a shallow grave in Highgate wood. It was raining heavily on the night she died and whoever killed her must have come away very dirty and muddy.."

"No shit, Sherlock," Paisley said impatiently, stubbing out his cigarette into an already overflowing ashtray. "Get to the point, if you have one." Evans stood her ground. She wanted very much to redeem herself for her mistake with the reporter. "When Sergeant Dukes interviewed her father, he noted that his shoes were all highly polished, and all his clothes had just come back from the dry cleaners."

"So?"

"Well, wouldn't you polish your shoes and have your clothes cleaned if you had evidence to hide?"

"We checked it out. The dry cleaner said he is a regular customer. It was nothing unusual. Gregg Green is a dapper man, very particular about his appearance."

"I know sir, but I had another look at the paper work. I realised I knew the dry cleaner, Mr Opodopolis. I use the same dry cleaners. Anyway, I took the liberty of popping in. Mr Opo was very helpful. He said he was going to contact us anyway. He found a pair of trousers that Gregg Green had not collected. On it was a note from the dry cleaners. It said they were unable to remove the stain on his trouser leg. It was embedded too deeply. The stain was a type of lichen. I ran a check. It only grows in dense woodland areas. The lichen is found in Highgate woods, where Louise' body was found."

Paisley looked murderous. "You have been a busy little bee haven't you?" he spat. "Why have you waited until now to inform me of this nugget? And why the fucking hell didn't anyone else on my team know about this?" He saw the crestfallen look on the keen young officer's face and his expression softened. She really was on the ball this girl, and as bright as the sun. He managed a grin and saw her spirits instantly lift. He added charitably, "Bloody good work, though girl!"

Victor sat in the prison waiting room and shifted uncomfortably. He had never been inside a prison before. He looked around as discretely as he could at the others waiting to visit loved ones. There were quite a few young women, some with children. Presumably waiting to see the poor kid's fathers. He wondered briefly, what crimes had been committed to make them end up here. He was beginning to wonder what he was doing here himself. Waiting to visit a murderer. He still could not believe it. He had always prided himself in being a pretty good judge of character. Then again, he mused, Billy Jameson had managed to fool all of them. He would never have thought big bluff gentle Gregg Green was capable of such a crime though. Strangling his own daughter. He shuddered involuntarily.

Jonny had been flabbergasted when he had told him quietly that he had received a visiting order from Gregg Green. He had been even more surprised when Victor had told him he intended to go. "What on earth do you want to see him for?" he had asked incredulously. Victor had paused for a bit, considering his answer. "I know it seems mad. Marlayna asked me the same question. I don't know, it's a terrible American expression, but what is it they say on all those law shows? Closure? Gregg and I, well, we go back a long way. I could not believe it when he was arrested. I was shocked to the core when he made a full confession. All those horrific headlines in the papers! I cannot believe he killed his own child like that. I think I just need to ask him why." Jonny sighed. "Well good luck, Dad. I don't think I'll ever be able to forgive him. God knows, I didn't like Louise, but to end up like that, dead In a ditch and murdered by her own father..." he let his voice trail off then said, "Well, for a while there I thought they were going to arrest me for it. I was petrified Dad. What with the police sniffing round and then those ruddy journalists! I'm just relieved it's all over. If you need to go and see Gregg, then you go. I just hope you don't make a habit of it."

Victor and the other people waiting were eventually allowed to go through to the visiting area. He had found the searches humiliating, but he realised how necessary they were. He had seen one woman carrying a toddler detained. The tot was screaming her head off now, poor little thing. A guard with a sniffer dog had told the woman that they needed to search the child's nappy. The young woman, who looked little more than a child herself, began swearing and protesting. "Get your fucking hands off me!" she screeched, "I told you I ain't got no fucking drugs!" Then she turned towards Victor and yelled "What you looking at? You nosy old bastard!"

Victor felt ashamed of how shocked he was. He had berated Jonny many times for being naïve, but here he was reacting in exactly the same way. He averted his eyes and followed the prison warden into the visiting area.

He did not recognise Gregg Green at first. He had lost a lot of weight and looked pale. He had never seen him dressed in anything other than a suit with a freshly ironed shirt and a waistcoat. It was incongruous seeing him in tracksuit bottoms, a tee shirt and a yellow prisoner's vest. He stood up when he saw Victor and managed a smile. "Thanks for coming" he said as Victor took a seat in the brightly lit communal area. "I did not expect you to come. It's very decent of you." Gregg continued. Now he was here, Victor did not know what to say. It was like visiting a sick person in hospital. He felt as if an invisible gag had been placed in his mouth like the bit on a horses bridle. It seemed to have him tongue-tied. After an awkward silence Victor said, "Shall I get us a drink?" there was a vending machine at the back of the room. Gregg nodded gratefully. "Yes please" he said, "Could I have a coffee? White with sugar, if it's not too much trouble."

As they sipped their drinks, Victor asked politely how Gregg was. Gregg smiled sadly. "I'm better than I deserve to be." He replied flatly. "I wanted to see you. I needed to apologise to you. I know you and Jonny have had a hard time because of me and..."he swallowed hard, "and..Louise." He sipped some more of his coffee. Victor swallowed his own drink. It was vile but he needed the caffeine. It was hot and very bitter but it gave him something to focus on. "I don't want any sympathy," Gregg announced bluntly. "Don't think I asked you to come here for that reason, Vic. I confessed because I could not live with myself any longer. I did not want anyone else being blamed for the terrible thing I did" Victor swallowed the last of his coffee. He put the plastic cup down on the little table in front of him. "Why on earth did you do it?" he blurted out eventually. Gregg did not seem surprised by the question. He was obviously expecting it. He rubbed his stubbly chin with his hand and leaned towards Victor. "I think for a while after I lost Marissa I lost my mind too." He said frankly. "I was so ashamed of Louise and what she had done. I went to the Barbican flat looking for her. I wanted her to come home with me, to put right all the horrible selfish things she had done. I never set out to hurt her…I swear. I had planned in my head what I was going to say to her, I just..I just wanted her to change. It was on impulse that I drove her to those woods." He stopped talking and smiled to himself. Victor sat silently opposite him. He had never seen Gregg Green unshaven before. He looked unkempt and slightly unhinged. It was very unnerving. Gregg coughed, clearing his throat. Then he continued, "We used to take her to the woods, Marissa and I, when she was just a little girl…she loved it there. I just wanted to talk to her. To make her understand… we always used to go to the woods if we needed to chat, it was so peaceful there, so relaxing. I wanted it to be the same as it was all those years ago, when we were a happy family and Marissa was healthy..but it all got out of control…I.. I got so angry with her. It was so frustrating, she did not understand, she kept screaming… I wanted to shut her up..I..I never smacked her, not when she was a child..maybe I should have been stricter, maybe if I had been she would not have turned into such a spoilt selfish brat.." he slumped back in his chair, looking utterly wretched. His eyes were full of tears and Victor felt a lump in his own throat. "I have lost everything" he whispered, "Everything I ever loved. This is the best place for me." He looked around at the other prisoners then took a tissue from his tracksuit pocket and blew his nose loudly. Then, abruptly, he stood up. Victor looked up at him in surprise. He held his hand out to Victor, and Victor, not knowing what else to do, shook it. "I want to go now." He said dismissively. "Thank you again for coming. It's not necessary to come again. I don't want or need visitors. I just wanted to...you know, say what I did. Goodbye Victor. I never deserved your loyalty or friendship. Please tell Jonny I am sorry for everything Louise put him through.Take care." He indicated to the prison guard that he wanted to go back to his cell.

Victor stood, speechless and bemused as the guard let Gregg Green away.

CHAPTER FOURTEEN

ONE YEAR LATER

Sarah and Suzy sat in the garden watching the children playing. It was a glorious sun splashed Sunday afternoon and Suzy and Jay were celebrating by throwing a barbecue party. Suzy looked around at the garden happily. This was her first ever garden. They had moved into Marlayna's house in Sekford Street only the month before. As if reading her thoughts, Marlayna came to join them. "How do you like your new home?" she asked, pulling up a chair and joining them, "Have you settled in okay?" Suzy beamed at her. "Oh, Mar, I'm so thrilled. I can't thank you enough. As you can see, the kids love the garden, and I can't get over the space. It seems enormous after our cramped little flat." Marlayna smiled. "I'm so thrilled for you. I am just sorry it took so long to get my horrible tenants out. I spoke to Cecilia next door, and she said she is so happy to have nice neighbours again. Your dad has worked wonders on the flowers. I'm so grateful to him."

"Aww, bless her. Cecilia is such a sweet heart. She's been ever so good. Amy loves her. She popped round with a cake on the day we moved in. Anyone who brings treats is always a hit with my two! They're already calling her Cissy, and she loves it! And my dad loves the garden. I don't know where he gets his knowledge from, he's never had more than a balcony." Marlayna raised her eyebrows in surprise. "He truly is amazing then. Those tomato plants look like prize winners. Cecilia said you gave her some veg yesterday too. She told me you help her with her shopping as well; it's very kind of you."

"It's the least I can do. I know her arthritis is bad at the moment. It's no bother. Me and Sarah sharing the work at the shop is ideal, so it's all worked out brilliantly. We both get to spend time with our kids, and you are a god send, Mar. How are you enjoying living upstairs?"

Marlayna laughed. "I've gone up in the world!" she winked. She and Victor had swapped their living arrangements around in the big house in Duncan Terrace. Sarah and Jonny had moved downstairs, and Victor and Marlayna had moved into Jonny and Sarah's flat upstairs. "It's worked out just fine." Marlayna said, smiling happily. It made perfect sense. I don't know why I didn't think of it before. The children have easy access to the garden, and we did not need all the space downstairs. It was silly when Jonny and Sarah were all squashed in with the children in the little upstairs flat"

Marlayna had suggested it to Victor one evening. "I did not like to mention it before. Because.. well, you know, I wondered if it would bring back painful memories?" Marlayna had said softly to Victor over dinner. He had looked perplexed.

"Why, because that bastard Billy stabbed me up there?" he had said bluntly between mouthfuls of fish pie. Marlayna had nodded. "No, I think it's a fantastic solution." Victor said, taking a gulp of his white wine. I was worried that they might decide to up sticks and move away completely, to tell the truth. They are squashed in like sardines up there now the kids are getting bigger. I'd be heartbroken if they went somewhere else." Marlayna clapped her hands together in delight. "Eat up then and let's go up and tell them. "

Sarah said to Suzy and Marlayna, "We are loving it downstairs. Jonny keeps teasing Victor and asking him if he can manage the stairs and Vic keeps having to thump him, but other than that, it's been an ideal move." She spotted Lydia trying to lift up her baby brother. "Lyddy, put Elli down!" she bellowed.   Little Elliot was almost walking. He was small for his age, but was catching up with the other one year olds in his toddler group. He had been pulling himself up on the furniture for a week or so. Sarah knew it would not be long before he took his first wobbly steps. Sarah and Jonny had both been worried that he might have some long term health problems due to being born prematurely. The hospital paediatrician had reassured them both that he was a perfectly healthy baby though. He was certainly bright and active and in to everything. Sarah lifted him into her arms and kissed his face. He chuckled happily. "What's that sister doing to you, eh?" she said. Lydia stood with her hands on her hips. "Mum, we're playing schools. I was only being the teacher." Sarah smiled at her daughter. "All right, madam." She said jokingly. "Just be careful." Lydia picked up the picture book that was on the edge of the sand pit. "Mum, I'm waiting to do the register. Can I have Elli back now? Or I'll just have to mark him absent." Sarah put the squirming baby gently down. Amy held his

hands. "Don't worry, I'll take care of him." She said Importantly. Then she added, "I'm the head teacher." Sarah left them to their game.
Bobby Jay was sitting obediently cross legged on the path, waiting for his lesson to begin. Shady the dog was sitting next to him, wagging her tail and looking adoringly up at Lydia.
Suzy and Marlayna were trying not to laugh. "They all get on so well." Marlayna said fondly, "It's lovely to see them playing so happily together." Suzy sipped her drink that Jay had just brought her. He was helping Jonny and Victor fire up the barbecue. He was on bar duty at the moment though.
"The boys have no choice but to play nicely." Suzy said, laughing. "Not with the two little miss bossy boots lauding it over them."
Next door Cecilia smiled as she heard the happy chatter over the garden wall. She was about to go and join them. She could not think of a better way to spend a Sunday afternoon than with her new friends. It was such a relief to have some civilised neighbours. Marlayna was an absolute angel, she had been so sorry when she left to move in with her handsome new partner. He was a lovely man, was Victor, and she was glad to see Marlayna happy, even though she missed her smiling face and the chats they used to have. That no good rude ex-husband of hers had led her a merry dance. Good thing she had come to her senses and kicked him into touch. It was just a worry when she decided to rent out the house. Having new neighbours move in was always an anxious time. Ben and Jemma had been fine though. She had liked them. They kept themselves to themselves and never caused any trouble. They had been there for a year or so and she had got used to them. She had been very anxious when they moved out. She just had one of her feelings about the new lot who took their place. Ben had been made redundant and got a new job in Birmingham. She had been right to be anxious. The new tenants had loud parties and played their music until all hours. She had asked them politely but it made no difference. She had had to phone Marlayna on numerous occasions about them. She didn't like to trouble anyone, but it really was intolerable. She couldn't rest. She never knew who was hanging about outside and they were rude to her too. It had got so bad she had been afraid to leave her house. Marlayna had told her she would not be renewing their lease. It had been a big weight off her shoulders, hearing that news. They had not wanted to go,

it had been a battle to get rid of them, but oh, it was such a relief when they finally left. Especially when Marlayna told her that a really nice family would be moving in. A family Marlayna knew very well and who she promised would cause no trouble. They had turned out to be perfect. They had their two darling little children too. Little Amy was such a sweet girl, and young Bobby Jay was such a happy little boy. You could always tell when children had been brought up properly. They didn't go around shouting and screaming like some of the rough kids she saw. She loved to hear them laughing and playing in the garden. It had turned into a happy home again and she was finally sleeping easy in her own bed at night. Jay was always there in the evenings and she felt safe knowing good people were just next door if she needed them. They had told her if she ever needed anything, she had only to ask. They had been good as their word, too. In just the few weeks they had been there, young Suzy had been really helpful, and even her dad had cut her grass and cleaned her windows. Such nice people were a rarity these days. She hoped they would stay for a very long time. She sighed happily.

She picked up her handbag and the cake she had made specially and went to join the party.

Nina called out to Adam "Are you finished in the bathroom? You take longer than me in there!"

Adam appeared at last. He waved his hand up and down his torso. "This kind of perfection takes a lot of effort." he said, winking at her. "Come on, we've not got all day," he added wickedly, and ducked as she tried to thump him playfully. They left the flat in Granville Square and made their way to the barbeque. "I can't wait to see their faces when we tell them we're getting married" Adam grinned at Nina as they got to the car. She smiled and kissed Adam's cheek. "Nor can I" she said, "I'll try not to dazzle too many people when I wave my engagement ring at them!" She could not resist waving her left hand in front of her so she could see the sparkle in the sunlight. Adam had whisked her off just the day before to choose it from Hatton Garden. Nina pondered as she wiggled her finger in the sun's rays how close she had come to losing everything. They had just arrived back home yesterday and Adam had nipped off to the Off license to get them a bottle of bubbly to celebrate.

When the doorbell had rung moments after Adam left, Nina had thought it was Adam, forgetting something. She had opened the door grinning but her face had fallen like a landslide when she opened the door. Nico had been standing on the doorstep. Had he been following her? She had not seen him since she had chucked him out of her flat. It seemed another lifetime ago now. He had avoided her in the hotel, much to her relief. She was shocked to see him standing there, and surprised that she did not feel even the slightest twinge. He had no power over her now. He looked a little older. Still as distinguished as ever although his black hair was greying slightly at his temples. He had asked if he could come in. She could not believe his cheek. He had actually reached for her hand. Then he had noticed her engagement ring. "Where did you get that from, a Christmas cracker?" he had said scathingly. It had been at this point that Adam had arrived. His face was set in fury as he took in the scene. "No, actually I bought it for her. Do you mind telling me what the hell you're doing on my doorstep?" Adam had smiled. It was a smile that said don't mess with me sunshine. Nina had felt her heart flip over and she realised just how much she loved Adam. "It's fine, Adam" she had said curtly, "This man is just leaving. He has nothing I want." Nico had tried to protest but Adam had pushed past him and said through gritted teeth, "Push off mate. You're not wanted here anymore"

When they had closed the door on Nico, Nina had flung her arms around Adam. He had embraced her, but had quickly pushed her away, just a little to search her face. "Are you sure you want to wear that Christmas cracker of a ring? I really need to know," he had whispered hoarsely. By way of reply, Nina had kissed him hard on the lips. "I have never been surer of anything in my entire life, Adam Sandford. I love you with all my heart." Her eyes shone and Adam held her then.

Adam nudged her gently and brought her back to reality. She had been lost in the memory and was staring at her beautiful ring. "Be careful there, Neen. You could blind someone with that glare. Come on, let's go and show that sparkler off. "

Rupert Bingly Warrington cleared away the leaves and tidied Louise's grave. He carefully laid the white roses he had brought beside the head stone. His eyes still misted when he read the inscription on the

182

headstone, which simply said, "Louise Blakely Green. Beloved daughter of Gregg and Marissa and Wife of Rupert. Taken too soon" He no longer felt angry at reading it. It had been his father in law, Gregg who had insisted the headstone used her maiden name. He had been hurt by that. Beloved daughter indeed! So beloved that he had lost his mind on that stormy night and strangled her. He still could not believe it. The news of His father in laws confession to the police had rocked him to his very core, even with all his training. He had thought himself unshockable. Thought he had seen it, heard it all. His own parents had been appalled by the whole grubby episode. His mother had berated him even now, for coming to London and visiting his wife's grave. She had sat and shuddered in her cashmere cardigan, dragging up all the sordid details over and over again. She had always been a terrible snob. She had told him that she wished he had never clapped eyes on any of "that family"

Rupert had managed to bite his tongue. It was no use arguing with his mother. She had lived all her life in the shelter of her wealth and privilege. She had married his father Gerald who had come from an equally privileged background. They had given Rupert the best education money could buy and had thought he had married well. The Blakely Greens were a well-respected family. Although Rupert had not done anything wrong, in his mother's eyes he had let the side down. Louise had not lived up to her expectations. She had brought scandal and worse, the press on to their doorstep. His mother had not once asked Rupert how he felt in all this. His reputation as a barrister had been tarnished and his heart broken. Despite everything, that she had put him through, he had truly loved Louise. He had clung on to the vain hope of reconciliation. When the police had told him she had been found dead he had been utterly destroyed. He was only now beginning to pick up the threads of his life. Her wretched father was safely behind bars and cliché or not, life did indeed go on. He had not yet found anyone else, and he doubted if he ever would trust another woman completely, but he had begun to rebuild his career and was at least functioning again.

He stood up, and as an afterthought, he took one of the roses, knelt and placed it on the neighbouring grave.

He stood up again and bowed his head solemnly. The freshly dug soil had no headstone yet, just a temporary marker. It had been her last wish to be laid to rest beside her friend. Another one taken too soon, he thought sadly, as he laid the bloom on the cold earth. Camilla had been a better friend to Louise than she ever deserved. Still, he hoped they were both at peace now.
Reluctantly he turned and walked away.

PROLOGUE

Martin Crayford saw his mother waiting for him outside the prison gates. She was smiling and raised her hand to wave. She stood eagerly waiting for him on the other side of the road. He felt the sun on his face and he closed his eyes and tipped his head up to catch the rays. They were the first sunbeams he had felt as a free man for many years. He had hoped Adele would be here instead of his mother. He had written to her regularly but she had never replied. He did not know her address, but his welfare officer had said they would try to forward the letters. Maybe she had not received any of them. He hoped she was happy, wherever she was. He had wanted to apologise to her. He really needed her to understand that he had been ill, but he was better now. He had shown nothing but remorse for what he had put her through back then Since he had transferred to the secure unit. He wondered how Dennis was. He would be quite grown up by now. He had written to Jay Oakland too. He hoped that he had received the letter. The screws had assured him they would deliver it. His psychiatrist had told him it was important to tell those he had hurt how sorry he was. Martin had not wanted to believe he was mentally unstable when he was first banged up. His illness was a great source of embarrassment for him. At first, he had been in denial and had refused any kind of medication. He had often been violent towards other prisoners and the screws. He had been transferred to the secure unit then. They had put him with all sorts of nutters. That was criminal. He smiled at the irony.
It had been his cellmate Danny, who had persuaded him to cooperate. "You have to play the game son," he had told him. "If they think you are being a good boy, if you tell them how sorry you are for what you did they'll let you out sooner and go easy on ya while yer 'ere." He had listened and taken in every word Danny had said. He had been a reformed character since then.

Martin grinned. He had never felt better. He was fit and well. He had made full use of the gym facilities while he was incarcerated. His voices told him he was invincible. He dropped the bag containing his medication in the litterbin and crossed the road to greet his smiling mother.

Printed in Great Britain
by Amazon.co.uk, Ltd.,
Marston Gate.